THE FAMILY
BUSINESS

INGRAM®

THE FAMILY BUSINESS

How Ingram Transformed the World of Books

KEEL HUNT

WEST
MARGIN
PRESS

To the generations of all our families,
Whose stories are told on these pages

Text © 2021 by Keel Hunt

Edited by Kristen Tate
Proofread by Dylan Julian
Indexed by Sheila Ryan
Layout by Jane Damiani

Library of Congress Cataloging-in-Publication Data is on file.
ISBN: 9781513295602 (paperback) | 9781513267210 (hardbound) | 9781513289595 (e-book)

Proudly distributed by Ingram Publisher Services

LSI 2021

Published by West Margin Press®

WEST
MARGIN
PRESS

WestMarginPress.com

WEST MARGIN PRESS
Publishing Director: Jennifer Newens
Marketing Manager: Angela Zbornik
Project Specialist: Micaela Clark
Editor: Olivia Ngai
Design & Production: Rachel Lopez Metzger

CONTENTS

FOREWORD

Tim O'Reilly
Founder, CEO, and Chairman of O'Reilly Media

When O'Reilly first began our unconventional publishing career in 1984, we'd never heard of Ingram, the largest wholesaler of books in the United States. O'Reilly was a technical writing consultancy, and we'd begun filling the gaps in our time by writing computer manuals that we thought needed to exist. Most of these were small books about individual Unix (later Linux) utility programs. We sold them by direct advertising in computer software magazines, at computer trade shows, and by licensing them to computer manufacturers who were distributing this new, industry-standard software.

All that changed in 1988, when we began publishing books explaining how to program the X Window System, a new graphical user interface layer for Unix. The books took off like hotcakes—we sold ten thousand copies of an unfinished two-volume set in six months, with the promise to deliver the final books when they were done. But more importantly, word spread, and bookstores (starting with Borders) began to demand our books. And that's how we first became an Ingram distribution partner when we already had over $7 million in publishing revenue.

We didn't have a salesforce. We didn't have any distribution agreements in place. But once the demand was there, this new channel exploded for us, largely because of the existence of the distribution network for which Ingram was the backbone. We often take companies like Ingram for granted; they are a mostly invisible part of how the economy operates. Yet the role they play is crucial for entrepreneurs and large companies alike. We experienced this enormous uplift to our business firsthand.

Because, of course, O'Reilly's 1992 book, *The Whole Internet User's Guide and Catalog*, by Ed Krol, went on to become a million-copy seller, and the book that introduced the World Wide Web to millions of software developers. There were only two hundred websites in existence when we first published the book; within a few years, there were millions. We went on to publish many other how-to books about Internet technologies, and several dot-com billionaires told us that they'd built their companies with the aid of our books. In 2000, when the cover of *Publishers Weekly* read "The Internet Was Built with O'Reilly Books," everyone took it as a simple statement of fact.

I tell this story because of the contrast with our next entrepreneurial journey. In 1993, O'Reilly launched the first-ever commercial, ad-supported website, the Global Network Navigator, or GNN. GNN was an online magazine and catalog that preceded Yahoo! by about a year, a portal providing access to the emerging world of the web.

The contrast with our explosive success as a publisher couldn't have been more striking. While Ingram and Borders had turbocharged our entry into an existing distribution ecosystem, no such ecosystem existed yet for the web. To help bring GNN to the world, we built our own web browser; we launched a combined software and information product called Internet in a Box, which contained dialup Internet software, access to GNN, and Ed Krol's *Whole Internet* book, to help people get onto the Internet; we worked in vain to make deals with telephone companies to provide Internet access; we commissioned the first-ever telephone survey on the prospects for advertising on the Internet, dialing up fifty thousand randomly selected consumers to try to prove to advertisers that if they came, demand would be there. Everything had to be invented and built from scratch.

I was struck by how different our experience was in publishing from our experience as Internet entrepreneurs. In one case, the existing infrastructure greased the wheels of our expansion; in the other, we had to do everything ourselves.

All of this makes me appreciate Ingram even more deeply. This is a company that has always served its partners, growing as we grow, and never at our expense.

Print publishing is a much smaller part of O'Reilly's business today (though Ingram delivers a far larger part of it, particularly since 2000, when O'Reilly president Laura Baldwin made a deal with John Ingram to switch us over to print-on-demand using Ingram services—another example of the transformative power of Ingram's infrastructure investments). Today, the largest part of our business is O'Reilly's online learning platform, a subscription-based digital marketplace for over forty-five thousand business and technical books, thirty thousand hours of video, live online training, interactive coding environments, technology certifications, and more, provided by hundreds of content partners and used by five thousand enterprise clients.

In managing this marketplace, we continue to take our inspiration from Ingram's generous enablement of its partner ecosystem, even as we use technologies from the digital realm like machine learning and personalization to help our customers navigate the best and most useful content and learning experiences provided both by our own team and by our partners.

At O'Reilly, one of our mottos is "Create more value than you capture." I like to think that we learned to think that way at least in part because of our long partnership with Ingram.

Another lesson we learned from Ingram is the need for constant reinvention. When we first began working with them, distribution of books, software, and music was all a matter of moving physical goods; today, the bulk of distribution is digital. Yet Ingram somehow thrived through the transition and has helped its partners also thrive. Reading this history, I learned how the company's process of constant reinvention began long before the current era. This is a story rich in both inspiration and practical lessons for any business that intends to stick around for the long haul.

INTRODUCTION

The first Ingram I ever met was Martha.

The year was 1981. Martha Ingram, the wife of E. Bronson Ingram, Chairman of Ingram Industries Inc., had come to the governor's office to pitch a new program for the Tennessee Performing Arts Center (TPAC) in Nashville. I was then a special assistant to Governor Lamar Alexander, and so it fell to me and a fellow staffer to greet Mrs. Ingram on the first floor of the state capitol.

By this date, Martha had already spearheaded the development of the downtown arts center, leading that project through eight long years of advocacy involving three different state administrations, multiple legislatures, layers of complex organization, and much fundraising. She had also, the previous year, presided over TPAC's triumphant grand opening.

On this visit, her ask was more modest: TPAC needed $25,000 to establish a program she would call Humanities Outreach in Tennessee (later renamed TPAC's Season for Young People). It would provide free tickets to students, from preschool through high school, to attend TPAC performances. Martha believed this would not only give the children broadening experiences with theater and music concerts but, in time, might also create new generations of patrons. The grant was soon approved, and the first performance under the auspices of the new program was Tennessee Williams's *The Glass Menagerie*, produced and directed by Mac Pirkle (who in 1985, with Martha, would cofound the Tennessee Repertory Theatre, now called the Nashville Repertory Theatre).

This began my introduction to the Ingram family, and eventually to their family businesses and their record of philanthropy. I would meet Martha's husband Bronson, then their son John Ingram and his siblings Orrin, Robin, and David. Later on, I would meet Martha's brother and sister in Charleston, South Carolina, and Bronson's siblings in Nashville. And over time, I came to know the sweep of the Ingram family's story, both in business and in their transformative philanthropy.

To this day, nearly four decades later, a recurring scene in downtown Nashville is the long lines of big yellow school buses parked bumper to bumper, circling the blocks around TPAC and the capitol. Their young passengers from schools across middle Tennessee are sitting inside the theaters, enjoying live performances of music and drama, perhaps for the first time in their lives—all as Martha had once envisioned.

This book tells the story of how the Ingram family, through its privately owned corporation, Ingram Industries, has transformed the global book publishing business. It focuses on the portion of Ingram Industries that is now called the Ingram Content Group, which celebrated its fiftieth year in 2020. Over this dynamic period, Ingram's book business has grown from a small regional supplier of books to Tennessee schools, libraries, and bookstores into an international concern, producing technological breakthroughs and innovative services that have led companies all over the world to rely on Ingram as a key player in the creation, production, distribution, and sale of books and other forms of intellectual content.

It's important to note that, in this book, the Ingram Content Group's older sister business, Ingram Marine Group, is mentioned only briefly. Ingram Marine has its own rich history of innovations and team building as the leader in the US inland marine industry, and it celebrated its fiftieth birthday in 1996.

Ingram Content Group's fiftieth year of operation has been no ordinary year. In 2020, Ingram Industries, like practically every business, found its usual operations seriously disrupted by the COVID-19 pandemic that was sweeping the world. But the Ingram Content Group discovered that its particular services were in unusually high demand, chiefly because of Ingram's sophisticated capacity for producing and shipping books (and other products) to distant places, reliably and quickly. In fact, while much of the world economy was shutting down in the wake of the pandemic, Ingram was running faster than ever to provide goods and services that millions of people and countless institutions relied upon. Here are three examples:

Amazon. In early March 2020, when the magnitude of the pandemic was just becoming clear, the big online retailer had to shift much of its own daily shipping work to the delivery of health-related products to millions of homes. Amazon called on Ingram to shoulder a larger share of its normal volume of book deliveries to consumers worldwide.

Textbooks. Ingram's VitalSource, a major provider of online textbooks, joined with its publisher partners to provide over fifty thousand digital textbooks to students in colleges and professional schools across the United States, Canada, and the United Kingdom—all free of charge—so they could finish the school semester despite pandemic-driven shutdowns.

Mayo Clinic. Called upon to produce an accelerated pandemic response that included tools for rapidly preparing nurses to serve the nation's overflowing hospitals, the famed health care providers turned to Ingram's Intrepid, the VitalSource corporate learning platform. Very quickly, Intrepid's platform and processes were used to certify more than three thousand nurses in COVID-19 care. This also was done at no charge, either to the Mayo Clinic or the nurses.

These are just three examples among many that illustrate the power and value of the business capabilities that Ingram Content has developed over its fifty years in operation.

How did a tiny, Tennessee-based book wholesaler turn into an international giant with such unique business capabilities? This book explains how it happened.

* * *

THE IDEA FOR THIS BOOK began over lunch in May 2018.

John Ingram had invited about a dozen people, including Ingram executives, a few retirees from the company, Martha Ingram, Mike Shatzkin, and me, to join him in the dining room at the company's Nashville headquarters. John raised the discussion topic: how best to observe the company's fiftieth anniversary, which would occur two years hence. In this meeting, it was Mike who suggested that a book might do justice to the true story behind Ingram Content Group. I was asked to take on the task.

This collection of mainly untold stories—about personalities and decisions, markets and dynamics, remarkable successes and a few failures—is told here with the full cooperation of John Ingram, his family, and his executive team. All told, there have been interviews with seventy-nine individuals who lived the story as it unfolded over the course of five decades. Telling what heretofore has remained publicly untold would have been impossible, of course, without the participation of these family members, executives, and associates, as well as many other stakeholders throughout the book industry.

The title of this book is intended as an homage to several types of family, in the various meanings of that word across our culture and especially in business.

First, the story of Ingram Content Group obviously begins with Ingram's founding family, and the choices and decisions they made along the way over a half-century of growth, struggle, and innovation that has changed an industry.

Second, there is the way in which this particular privately held business and its leaders have instilled a special camaraderie among its own workforce. In this book, you'll learn how Ingram has fostered a family spirit among its associates, an all-hands-on-deck ethos of cooperation, and a norm of mutual regard and respect for colleagues, all above and beyond the usual commitment to businesslike performance of tasks and assignments. Today more than four thousand people work at Ingram and participate in its extraordinary corporate culture. There are valuable lessons that business leaders and students may learn from its story.

Third, more broadly there is the living phenomenon of a family business and all that that means in our broader culture. A family business, whatever its name or business category, is usually a special business. Some endure longer than others. Family members may share the vision behind a successful enterprise, and they may pass its ownership and control down to successive generations, or they may not. And yet the dynamics behind any business owned by any family are always unique to that particular front office. Ingram's story is one of these, and it represents some of the very best qualities that outstanding family businesses have to offer.

It's my hope that the stories in this book, covering a half-century of innovation, experimentation, and growth, may be a respectful salute not only to the generations of the Ingram clan and their team, but also to all family businesses large and small, and to the entrepreneurs, intrapreneurs, risk-takers, and visionaries who come in all sizes, across time and all sectors. They are the optimists who create not only jobs but the future. In ways large and small, they activate, sustain, and enrich our economy and communities each day. It is their struggles and triumphs that do so much to drive America forward.

Keel Hunt
Nashville, Tennessee
August 2020

PART ONE
The Beginning

1
The Family

The Ingram story was not always about books and publishers, booksellers and libraries, authors and readers. In its earliest American generations, the Ingram family was rooted in the timber industry of the Northeast and Midwest.

A young Orrin Henry Ingram emigrated from Leeds, England, in the early 1800s. He worked first in western Massachusetts. Then, in 1850, he decamped to Ontario, where he became a manager in the lumber mills. Seven years later, he resettled his family in Eau Claire, in western Wisconsin. An entrepreneur at heart, O. H. Ingram cofounded his own company in the highly competitive young timber industry centered on the vast river system of the Upper Mississippi.

In 1881, Ingram was a central figure in the organizing of six competing lumber mills, including his own, into the Empire Lumber Company, part of a giant timber business being built by Frederick Weyerhaeuser. Later headquartered in the Pacific Northwest, the Weyerhaeuser organization became a preeminent vendor of construction timber and, for a time, America's largest landowner. O. H. Ingram became a close associate of Frederick Weyerhaeuser as well as a partner and shareholder in the burgeoning enterprise.

By the 1920s, the timber business in Wisconsin was in decline. In 1928, the grandson of O. H., another Orrin Henry Ingram, generally known as Hank, bought a Nashville textile business called the Tennessee Tufting Company. Hank Ingram had recently married the former Hortense Bigelow, a member of one of the most prominent families in St. Paul, Minnesota. Now he brought his young bride to live with him in Tennessee's capital city. Thus began a mutually beneficial connection between Nashville and the Ingram family that continues to this day.

By 1936, Hank Ingram had reorganized his business into an entity called the Ingram Manufacturing Company, with two subsidiaries—Ingram Spinning

Company, which produced merino yarn, and Tennessee Tufting Company, which made tufted fabrics. He had also become a director of the Tennessee Railway and a member of the advisory board of American National Bank—all by the age of thirty-two.

The fabric business remained part of the Ingram family holdings until the 1960s. But by the late 1930s, Hank Ingram felt the need to examine other business opportunities. He became interested in oil exploration and refining, an industry that had struggled during the Great Depression but that was being revived by the gradual economic recovery as well as the looming threat of war in Europe. In 1939, in partnership with two other businessmen, Ingram launched the Wood River Oil and Refining Company and built a refinery at Wood River, Illinois, not far from St. Louis. At the time, oil pipelines used to transport petroleum products were not widespread, so refinery companies had to make use of rail, truck, and boat transportation networks instead. To improve his company's delivery service to customers, Ingram and his partners launched the Wood River Oil Barge Company in 1942, which set about building a fleet of river barges.

When the United States entered World War II in 1941, the demand generated by the war effort helped spur rapid growth for the Ingram oil and refining operations. They continued to grow for the next two decades. A big new refinery with modern equipment and dock facilities was built in New Orleans in 1954, and in 1955 the newly organized Ingram Barge Company took over management of the fleet of barges, which was busier than ever with oil deliveries.

By the early 1950s, Hank Ingram had become a prominent figure in Nashville's business circles. He was also an important donor to Vanderbilt University, where he served as a member of the university's Board of Trust from 1952 until his death in 1963. This began a generations-long relationship between the Ingram family and Nashville's largest university. Hank and Hortense also had a growing family, with four children: Fritz (born in 1929), Bronson (1931), Alice (1933), and Patricia (1935).

During the early 1940s, the Ingram family lived part of the time in St. Paul, where Hortense Ingram had grown up. In fact, Fritz and Bronson, the first two Ingram children, were born in St. Paul, and Bronson attended St. Paul Academy from 1941 to 1942. But the harsh Minnesota winters finally convinced Hank Ingram that Nashville was the best place to raise his family. They settled year-round in Tennessee, although Hank and Hortense kept a summer home on White Bear Lake in Minnesota until Hortense's death in 1979.

Bronson Ingram, the second child of Hank and Hortense, would eventually become his generation's most significant leader of the Ingram family businesses.

Young Bronson spent one year at the prestigious Phillips Andover Academy in Massachusetts, but he was so homesick for Tennessee that his parents agreed to let him complete his secondary school education in Nashville. In 1949, he graduated from Montgomery Bell Academy, the venerable boys' preparatory school in Nashville that served as the model for the setting of the 1989 film *Dead Poets Society*. (Thomas Schulman, the screenwriter, was a Montgomery Bell alum.)

Bronson's longtime friend Jake Wallace describes him as intense and pugnacious. "He was forever getting into fights... although he lost more often than he won," Jake recalls. And despite being raised in privileged circumstances as part of a successful business family, Bronson was unusually self-disciplined and hardworking. He was also disdainful of others who didn't dedicate the same level of energy and intensity to their efforts, whether in work, school, or sports.

Bronson became an avid and highly competitive sailor, and followed his father's lead in becoming a serious golfer. Bronson's love of that sport would later lead to a longtime friendship with the legendary golfer Arnold Palmer, whom he met in 1959 at the New Orleans Country Club. Ultimately Arnold and his wife Winnie would travel all over the world with Bronson Ingram and his wife Martha, playing golf and enjoying one another's company.

A family friend, the Nashville banker Sam Fleming, who became something of a mentor to Bronson, lists a series of traits that Bronson shared with his father:

> Both got upset, but didn't stampede when things went wrong, but rather grew stronger and more determined to work things out and usually did... When they were upset, they had a short fuse, usually expressed in some profanity... Both had great integrity. *Dictum Meum Pactum* (translated "My Word Is My Bond") has been the motto of the London Stock Exchange. It most assuredly would apply to both Hank and Bronson throughout their entire lifetimes.

After finishing high school in 1949, Bronson attended Vanderbilt for a year, then transferred to Princeton, where he graduated in 1953 with a degree in English. He then spent two years in the US Navy, serving on the attack transport ship USS *Cambria* in the Mediterranean.

In 1955, Bronson joined the family business, the Ingram Products Company. His main focus was the Ingram Oil and Refining Company, which by then had launched a network of fifteen company-owned retail gas service stations in five states. Bronson set to work becoming an "oil man," steeped in the distinctive tradition and culture of an industry that had long played a dominant role in the economies of states across the American South.

Bronson also devoted time and energy to a budding social life. Tall, athletic, good-looking, and with a promising career ahead of him, he was widely considered one of Nashville's most attractive young bachelors.

In 1957, while visiting New York, he met Martha Robinson Rivers, a native of Charleston, South Carolina, who was a senior at Vassar, smart and energetic, and a vivacious, lovely young woman—just as much of a catch as Bronson. In company with a group of friends, the two spent a weekend enjoying the glamour of the big city, traveling in limousines to performances of *My Fair Lady* with Rex Harrison and Julie Andrews and hearing Édith Piaf sing at a nightclub.

Bronson and Martha quickly developed an attraction that turned into a serious courtship. Bronson would often visit with Martha by flying to Charleston in the Ingram company plane, a twin-engine Cessna 310. In the memoir Martha wrote about Bronson decades later, she recalls that the Cessna often developed mysterious "mechanical difficulties" that required Bronson to stay overnight for a second day with Martha.

Bronson and Martha were married in Charleston on October 4, 1958. For two-and-a-half years, they lived in New Orleans, where the Ingram Corporation was headquartered. In 1961, they moved to Nashville. By this time, they had also started their own family. Their son Orrin H. Ingram was born in 1960; John R. Ingram was born in 1961; and David B. Ingram came along in 1962. Daughter Robin arrived in 1965.

In time, Martha Ingram would become Nashville's preeminent patron of the arts. In addition to her campaign to develop TPAC and her role in cofounding the Tennessee Repertory Theatre, she has been a leading donor and supporter of other prominent performing arts organizations in Tennessee's capital city, as well as in her hometown of Charleston, South Carolina. She served as board chair of the Nashville Symphony and was the prime civic mover behind the development of Nashville's Schermerhorn Symphony Center, which opened its doors in 2006. At the same time, Martha was also using her talents to play an important role in the success of the Ingram family business, as we'll explain later in these pages.

In 1961, Ingram Oil and Refining Company was merged with the larger Murphy Oil, which took over management of the combined operations. This appeared to mean that Bronson's budding career as an oil man was at an end. He and his brother Fritz bought part-ownerships in various businesses, some of which flopped—for example, a company that made wax coating for milk cartons, which they invested in just before that material was superseded by plastic coating. Bronson also started a fiberglass boat-building company, Superglas Corporation, which succumbed to intense competition in that industry. These setbacks didn't seem to discourage Bronson. If anything, they reinforced what appears to have been an instinctive understanding of the importance of experimentation, flexibility, and resilience in business. Trying anything new involves an unavoidable element of risk. If it fails, you learn from the experience and then try something else. Bronson would operate according to this philosophy for the rest of his life, and it became a lasting hallmark of the larger Ingram enterprise.

By 1962, a newly formed Ingram Corporation had been launched. It was soon operating two businesses. Ingram Materials Company purchased the assets of Cumberland River Sand and Gravel Company, and then, in 1963, Ingram Corporation bought a barge company called Barrett Line. These businesses would later provide a springboard for the family's return to the oil industry. Bronson was brought on board to work alongside his father Hank in managing some of these family businesses, while older brother Fritz was in New Orleans, running portions of the Ingram businesses that were based in that city while also pursuing separate business interests of his own.

Bronson had been learning about business directly from his father for some eight years when a shocking event occurred. While on a visit to New Orleans, late one night in April 1963, Bronson and Martha got a call telling them that Hank had died suddenly of an aneurysm. He was only fifty-eight years old.

At the age of thirty-one, Bronson found himself thrust into the role of leading the Ingram Corporation. It was a job he'd expected to fill one day, but not so soon.

2
The Favor

Taking over leadership of the family businesses in the wake of his father's untimely death might have been a daunting challenge for Bronson Ingram, but he quickly proved himself equal to the task.

During the 1960s and 1970s, Ingram Corporation grew and expanded steadily. While maintaining the Ingram Barge and Ingram Materials businesses, the company became involved in ocean transportation, petroleum exploration, oil and gas pipeline construction, and service subsidiaries for the oil industry. Many of these businesses were capital-intensive, calling for significant investments in machinery. Ingram's reach was also global, including derrick barges, offshore oil platforms, and pipelines in Indonesia, the Gulf of Mexico, the Bahamas, Brunei, and Australia. Towboats and barges owned by Ingram plied the United States' inland waterways, carrying cargo from state to state. (Many of these vessels were named after Ingram family members—for example, the towboat *Martha R. Ingram* was christened in New Orleans in June 1971. Other boats have been named in honor of Ingram board members, Ingram executives and other long-term valued associates, and leaders of commercial banks with whom Ingram has done business.)

In 1974, Ingram subsidiary Great Plains Construction Company became a major participant in the building of the Trans-Alaska Pipeline. And in the same year, Ingram launched a joint partnership with Northeast Petroleum Industries to build a 200,000-barrel-a-day petroleum refinery near New Orleans. It was one of the largest privately financed refineries in the world, and the first refinery in the United States specially designed to handle the higher-sulfur crude oil produced in the Middle East. Known as Energy Corporation of Louisiana, the refinery was ultimately sold to Marathon Oil in September 1976.

These big industrial projects continued to build the wealth of the Ingram family and the reach of Ingram Industries under the stewardship of Bronson Ingram. But at the same time, a much less visible and seemingly insignificant corner of the Ingram family business was laying the foundation for an even more remarkable story of growth—set in a very different economic arena.

Ingram Industries' significant role in heavy industries like oil production and cargo hauling didn't make the company a natural platform for an extension into the very different world of book publishing. There was no obvious economic or managerial strategy behind the move. It all started, in fact, as just a favor—an act of kindness by a wealthy oil man to a retiring college administrator named Jack Stambaugh.

In 1956, after a career in business and government, including service in the Eisenhower administration, Stambaugh was hired to be Vanderbilt University's vice chancellor for business affairs. Soon after moving to Nashville, he met Hank Ingram, who had been elected to the Vanderbilt Board of Trust just four years earlier. For seven years, Ingram and Stambaugh were close friends, talking regularly about higher education, business, and life in Nashville.

When Hank Ingram died in 1963, his son Bronson was invited to take his father's seat on the Vanderbilt governing board. Like his father, he became deeply involved in the university's philanthropy and governance, and he got to know Jack Stambaugh as well.

In 1964, shortly before Stambaugh's retirement from the university administration, he met with Bronson to talk over some possible post-retirement business opportunities. This conversation led to Bronson offering Stambaugh an office at Ingram headquarters, so that he would have a place to "work" in retirement. The Ingram Corporation's offices were relatively small at the time; the company shared a low-rise commercial building on Harding Road, on the city's west side, with a branch office of Third National Bank on the street level. This location was only a dozen blocks west of the Vanderbilt campus (and quite close to the current Ingram headquarters, also on Harding Road).

For the first few months of his retirement, Stambaugh spent most days sitting at his new desk at Ingram headquarters, usually reading the *Wall Street Journal*. Observing Stambaugh's idleness, so uncharacteristic of his friend, Bronson suggested that he find a business to run. If they could agree on the prospect, Bronson said Ingram would buy half of the business and also provide financing for future growth.

Stambaugh agreed, and he soon returned to Bronson with an acquisition prospect: a business then called the Tennessee School Book Depository.

Textbook depositories were state government creations that had sprung up across the United States in the 1930s. Their purpose was to make it possible for local schools, particularly in the rural South, to get easier access to textbooks published by the major publishers mostly located in New York. These big companies weren't interested in serving tiny customers like small local schools or school districts. Textbook depositories represented the combined interests of local boards of education throughout a state, amplifying the buying power of individual districts as part of a broader statewide purchasing combine and making the warehousing and distribution processes more efficient. In accordance with state regulations, they also ensured that textbooks would be available whenever they were needed by creating in-state storage facilities for them.

In Ingram's home state of Tennessee, the legislature had established its own depository in 1935. Local districts continued to make their own textbook selections in keeping with the subject-area adoption cycles established by the State Board of Education. For a fee, the depository service would receive orders from the local systems, aggregate them, negotiate purchases with the various textbook publishers, and then coordinate timely deliveries back to the districts ahead of the start of each academic year. State government funding for all this was typically steady.

Bronson liked what he heard about this business. The depository represented a limited business but a reasonably steady one. Its customers, the local school districts, were deemed good credit risks. The business would be almost risk-free, and perhaps it would be possible to identify potential avenues for expansion. Even as a fledgling executive, Bronson Ingram had already developed the strong growth orientation that would guide his entire business career as well as a keen sense of the need to balance risk with opportunity.

After some discussion, Stambaugh approached the depository's founder and owner, Forest Reed, and learned that Reed was willing to sell. A meeting was quickly arranged with Bronson Ingram.

A longtime Ingram executive remembers Bronson telling him what happened next: "To figure out the offering price, he wrote a number down on a piece of paper and put it on the table. Mr. Reed wrote a number down on a piece of paper and put it on the table. When they turned the two pieces of paper over, they both said $245,000. And so that's what they paid to buy Tennessee School Book Depository."

Ingram set up the company with starting capital of $500,000 to cover the purchase price and seed funding to support ongoing operations and the pursuit of growth opportunities. They retained the business name, and Stambaugh took the office and operations base on Second Avenue North in downtown Nashville, then principally a commercial zone of warehouses.

In this way, Ingram Industries established a toehold in the book business. At the time, Bronson Ingram knew little about the world of publishing. It's doubtful he had any idea of how this modest investment would grow into a major part of the family's business, much less that it would ultimately help transform one of the world's most culturally significant yet economically challenged industries. But the stage had been set for all this to happen in the decades to come.

* * *

MILLIONS OF AMERICANS LOVE TO read books, but relatively few of them know much about how book publishing actually works. The process by which an author's words find their way into the hands of readers has evolved over hundreds of years since the German craftsman Johannes Gutenberg developed his technique for printing with moveable type in the mid-fifteenth century—one of the first and most important industrial innovations of the modern era. Moveable type made mass-produced books possible for the first time, sparking a revolutionary increase in middle-class literacy and the birth of the first modern marketplace for books.

By the twentieth century, the complex network of publishers, printers, authors, agents, wholesalers, booksellers, librarians, and others engaged in the task of producing books and making them available to readers was often referred to as "the book industry." But this is something of a misnomer because it implies that there's a single monolithic industry by that name. In reality, there are many "book businesses," defined by varying kinds of books, readers, markets, distribution systems, and other characteristics.

The various book businesses in the United States include:

- *Trade publishing*, which involves books of general interest aimed at ordinary readers. It gets its name from the original term for the array of independent booksellers found in almost every city around the United States—"the book trade." Chances are good that, when you think about book publishing, trade publishing comes to mind first. The legal thrillers of John Grisham, the *Harry Potter* fantasies of J. K. Rowling, Michelle Obama's memoir *Becoming*, the historical works of Doris Kearns Goodwin, and how-to books about diet and fitness, parenting, careers, and home improvement—all of these and more are examples of trade publishing.
- *Textbook publishing*, which produces books for use in schools by students at the elementary, middle school, high school, college, and graduate school levels. Each of these textbook categories has its own peculiar editorial and pedagogical requirements, sales and marketing methods, economic demands, and distribution channels, and so each can be considered a "book business" in its own right.
- *Scientific, technical, medical, and professional publishing*, which produces specialized books for practitioners in various fields of endeavor. Again, each class of books within this broad category has its own complicated set of content requirements as well as specialized sales and marketing channels that publishers must employ.

- *Academic and scholarly publishing*, which produces books by and for scholars and researchers, mostly those working in universities.
- *Religious publishing*, which produces books for members of specific faith communities (primarily, in the United States, Christian denominations), but also includes other types of religious books, such as Judaica.

Each of these has its own systems for identifying authors, deciding which books to publish, developing content, physically producing copies, marketing and advertising titles, and distributing them to readers. Specialized publishers, sales and marketing organizations, publicity experts, and booksellers have grown up to serve these varying businesses. Many of the processes involved appear arcane and arbitrary to outsiders and even to some of those engaged in publishing. In some cases, inertia and tradition have retarded efforts to modernize and reform the book businesses, leading to frustration for authors, publishers, booksellers, and readers alike. One fact that exacerbates this problem is that most of the individuals involved in publishing are drawn to the work because of their love of books rather than any fascination with business strategy or management. (A famous quip says that "the problem with book publishing is that it's made up of English majors trying to do math.")

Peculiarities specific to book publishing contribute to its complexity. For example, few industries involve the development and introduction of so many new, unique products. No one really knows the number of new book titles published in the United States every year, but it is clearly well into the six figures. Even individual publishing companies produce hundreds or thousands of different new books annually; at Simon & Schuster, for example, the number of new titles published averages about two thousand per year. The challenge of pushing this many unique new products through the sales and marketing pipeline, and of advertising, publicizing, and promoting them so that potential readers are aware of them, is almost incalculable. (Imagine the confusion and chaos if Coca-Cola, for example, tried to introduce hundreds of new flavors of Coke every single year!)

Then consider the fact that *older* books, the so-called backlist titles, actually constitute a major source of revenue for most publishers. HarperCollins, for example, publishes hundreds of new works of fiction every year, hoping to turn each one into a popular success that will sell thousands of copies. But year in and year out, HarperCollins actually earns far more of its corporate profits from a novel originally published in July 1960—Harper Lee's *To Kill a Mockingbird*, which sells an estimated 750,000 to one million copies annually.

Most successful publishers have a roster of backlist titles, including both fiction and nonfiction, that they rely on for much of their income. This means that, even as they labor to draw attention to hundreds or thousands of new products, publishers and their allies throughout the business, especially booksellers, must also devote time, space, energy, money, and other resources to keeping hundreds of significant backlist titles available and to marketing and promoting them in ways relevant to their current customers. It's a juggling act no other industry is forced to practice. (Imagine if General Motors was still manufacturing and selling a selection of classic cars from the '60s, '70s, and '80s alongside its brand-new models! Of course, GM does make replacement parts for those old vehicles available, which demands production and logistical resources, but no special sales, marketing, or promotional effort needs to be mounted on behalf of those thousands of parts.)

Further complicating matters is the relatively small size of the industry. One classic study of book publishing, Leonard Shatzkin's *In Cold Type*, estimated the total sales of the entire industry in 1982, including all the book categories previously listed, at around $6 billion, which the author noted was less than the sales of the Philip Morris Company alone. The basic picture has not changed much since then. In 2019, the US book publishing business had estimated revenues of just under $26 billion—which is less than Microsoft Corporation racked up that year *in a single quarter*. This means that, as compared with other industries, in book publishing, a very large number of products is chasing a relatively tiny amount of sales revenue.

When one considers the economic and strategic challenges faced by the book business, the fact that book publishers continue to operate profitably, generation after generation, might seem surprising. But, of course, there are millions of people, in the United States and around the world, who love books and couldn't imagine living without them. These booklovers constitute a dedicated market that has existed for centuries and will probably never disappear. No wonder there are always businesspeople interested in looking for ways to unlock the enormous economic value this sizeable audience represents. They include the savvy and experienced executives who head up the global media corporations that have come to dominate the American publishing scene over the last several decades. All of these smart businesspeople agree that there is plenty of potential profit to be made in book publishing.

Yet it remains true that the world of publishing presents a challenging business environment, to say the least—one in which finding the funds to innovate, modernize, and grow the business is not easy.

* * *

THIS, THEN, WAS THE UNFAMILIAR business environment into which Bronson Ingram had stuck a toe in 1964.

The Tennessee Book Company occupied just a tiny niche in the relatively small and highly diverse book business. At the time, the entire US textbook market would have represented less than a billion dollars in sales, and the Tennessee Book Company's role was that of an industry intermediary in just a single, modest-sized southern state. At a glance, any prospects for dramatic growth would be hard to discern.

However, as managed by Stambaugh under Bronson's watchful eye, Tennessee Book Company grew slowly but steadily over several years, though on a smaller scale compared to the other Ingram businesses. As Bronson had realized, the company's business model was almost risk-free. Unlike the trade book business, the textbook business features a market that is highly predictable in size and scope. Census data reveal with great accuracy the number of students in any given age cohort, and these students represent a captive audience for the products created by the textbook publishers. If, say, sixty thousand middle school students in a state are required to study algebra in a given year, then it's a near certainty that sixty thousand algebra textbooks will be needed; popular tastes or fashions won't impact sales as they do with the trade book bestseller lists.

Within the statewide slice of the textbook industry that Tennessee Book Company served, there was rarely any interruption in the legislature's recurring annual appropriations for new textbook adoptions. Even the occasional political skirmish over a controversial title within local school boards was rare and, in any event, well beyond the purview of the depository, which was merely a wholesale distributor, not a policymaker.

So the Tennessee Book Company was a relatively simple piece of the broader Ingram Corporation landscape. Most of Bronson's time and attention was necessarily focused on the bigger Ingram businesses, from Ingram Barge Company to the prospering oilfield distribution company called Ingram Petroleum Services. But Bronson did pay attention to the book business. He conducted biweekly "ops review" meetings with Stambaugh, just as he did with the top executives across all his profit centers. And he encouraged Stambaugh to find ways to pursue growth.

Seeds of growth for Ingram's role in the book industry were quietly being planted—seeds that, in the years to come, would grow beyond anyone's expectations.

3

Stirrings of Growth

The core business of Tennessee Book Company was the textbook depository services it provided to local school districts. But even before the business was purchased by Ingram, it had developed some small sidelines that added to its revenues and profits. For example, the company had been selling books to libraries—especially school libraries. In the mid-1960s, when President Lyndon Johnson's so-called Great Society social programs began pouring federal money into schools, including into school libraries, Bronson Ingram and Jack Stambaugh sensed a business opportunity, so they set about expanding the book company's library sales operations

Bronson also encouraged Stambaugh to begin hiring talented, knowledgeable people who could help identify and take advantage of growth opportunities for the book business. In many cases Bronson was personally involved in these hires. For example, in 1968, he helped recruit an executive who would become a pivotal person in the Ingram story—a smart, charismatic, and ambitious young sales and marketing manager named Harry Hoffman.

Hoffman had an unusual background. Back in the early 1950s, after graduating from Colgate University, the young Hoffman spent several summers working as a lifeguard on Jones Beach in the Long Island suburbs of New York. Then he joined the Federal Bureau of Investigation, sworn in by the director himself, J. Edgar Hoover. (Hoffman believed that one of the reasons he'd been hired was that Hoover had developed a penchant for enlisting *tall* agents: "When he came to greet us new recruits," Hoffman recalls, "we were all six feet three or taller. Hoover himself was a lot shorter, so he actually stood on a milk carton to address us.") Hoffman worked for six months at the Atlanta penitentiary, interviewing prisoners on behalf of the FBI, then spent a year in Washington, DC, keeping tabs on Russian military personnel stationed in the United States.

Hoffman was an ambitious young man; law enforcement didn't provide him with the kind of career challenges he craved. In 1954, Hoffman left the agency to seek opportunities in business. He worked with Procter & Gamble in New York for four years, then joined the optical manufacturing company Bell & Howell for the next seven, with assignments in North Carolina,

New York, Chicago, and Cleveland, eventually becoming Bell & Howell's director of marketing. He later worked for Demco, a Madison, Wisconsin–based firm that provided supplies and equipment to libraries and schools.

Though a young man still in his thirties, with modest managerial experience, Hoffman had already set his sights on becoming a high achiever in business. In his 1998 book *The Pocket Mentor*, Hoffman recalls how it happened:

> At the age of thirty-five, while I was still working for Bell & Howell, I came to the realization that I knew more about the business of selling and marketing cameras and projectors than my bosses did. It had taken me too many years to realize that just because a person occupies a position of power in a company, that person is not necessarily the best one for the position. I had always been intimidated by bosses and their power. Now, at thirty-five, I began to think that I might be as smart as (or smarter than) the people who directed me. I decided to change my approach.
>
> I went from being a somewhat passive person to being someone who could take on the responsibility of rocking the boat and making the changes that I thought would improve the company. I became much more assertive and told literally everyone in the company how I felt about the way things were going. My bosses implemented some of my ideas and liked the results. This earned me several promotions in rapid order, and for the first time in my life I had the confidence necessary to take the actions I felt would improve the way the companies I worked for did business.

A new Harry Hoffman had emerged—and this new personality would serve as the foundation for a dynamic career that would help transform not just Ingram's book business but the entire industry in which it played a part.

In 1968, Hoffman was lured away from Demco to the Tennessee Book Company by a headhunter he met at a library conference in Kansas City. "It was about a $500,000 business at the time," Hoffman recalls, "and the work was strictly in the fall, August through September." Hoffman saw opportunity in the story of this modest business. He and his wife Norma moved south to Nashville.

As the book company's new director of marketing, Hoffman set about working on expanding its schoolbook business. For example, he landed a contract to supply books to Louisiana state schools. Since the book company already had a large warehouse facility, expanding the market it served carried with it only modest costs while boosting both sales revenues and profits. This was the kind of steady, almost risk-free growth Bronson Ingram had hoped to see. In the decades to come, much of Ingram's profitable growth would depend on the same basic principle of leveraging a well-run physical infrastructure to provide valuable services to an ever-growing, steadily diversifying market of customers.

The Tennessee Book Company was showing signs of outgrowing its origins as a simple favor from one businessperson to another. Then, in 1969, a personal twist of fate would spell the end of those early days in the company's story.

In that year, Stambaugh's wife Helen became ill with emphysema. Soon thereafter, Stambaugh informed Bronson that her doctor was recommending long absences from Nashville's humid climate. Their plan would be to move to the drier US Southwest—which meant that Stambaugh would no longer be able to run the book company.

Bronson bought out Stambaugh's interest in the book company. Within a few months, the Stambaugh family would be gone from Tennessee. However, the legacy of the Stambaugh family is still remembered in Nashville, where it is fittingly intertwined with that of the Ingrams. Today on the east side of the Vanderbilt campus, there is a configuration of ten buildings called the Ingram Commons. It includes more recent residential quarters for first-year students and a student center with office spaces for faculty. One of these first-year residential halls is called Hank Ingram House, while another bears the name Stambaugh House.

But in 1969, Helen Stambaugh's illness, which posed a personal challenge for her family, created a business management dilemma for Bronson. He had to find new leadership for the tiny book company that had been quietly growing in an odd corner of his business portfolio.

Martha Ingram remembers Bronson sharing this sudden development with her at home one evening. "Now I'm left with this little book depository," he told her. "What in the hell am I going to do with it? I'm an oilman. That's what I do. I don't know anything about books. Now I've got this little business I've either got to look after or shut it down."

Bronson wasn't pleased to be faced with this new demand on his time and energy. He was already working an intense business schedule that included continual travel. Martha tells the story of how their young son John, during one period when Bronson was frequently on the road, asked her, "Mommy, do we still have a father?" The question moved Martha to demand that Bronson reorganize his life to allow more time with the family. "Of course, Bronson was pulled in a lot of different directions," Martha says. "He had a lot of business interests and he was an avid sportsman as well as a civic leader. He adored his children, but he left the job of raising them mainly to me."

Under the circumstances, for Bronson to shoulder a much larger role in running the book business would have been too much.

Fortunately, a possible solution was at hand in the person of Harry Hoffman. Bronson quickly focused on Hoffman as the book business's next leader. "I can teach him how to run the company. I think Harry will be able to do this just fine," he told Martha.

As the time for Stambaugh's departure drew near, Bronson promoted Hoffman to general manager and urged him to begin thinking about the book business more broadly. Bronson also began dedicating more of his own time and energy to making sure that the book business—now renamed the Ingram Book Company—was on sound footing and was pursuing a solid path toward growth.

"That was the beginning," Martha recalls. "After that, Bronson went out to this 'little book company' for at least half a day every week. He was focused on getting Harry to learn to be accountable for what came in and what went out, and the difference between costs and profits."

Hoffman was now in charge of the future of the Ingram Book Company. In 1970, the total employee head count stood at only eighteen. Total sales clocked in at about one million dollars per year. It was a small business by any standard. But Hoffman had already started developing some ideas for growing the company, and he had financial and management backing as well as insightful advice provided by a savvy business strategist, Bronson.

The initial growth strategy was a simple one: to identify potentially profitable activities that could be carried out using the existing resources of the Ingram Book Company. "We had this big warehouse, a huge warehouse," Hoffman recalls. "And I said, 'Well, why don't we see if we can sell to bookstores?'"

Bronson agreed that it was worth a try. Of course, this meant expanding the company's reach from one set of book businesses—the school textbook and school libraries businesses—into another book business with a different economic, marketing, sales, and distribution model—namely, the trade book business.

As products, school textbooks and trade books don't have much in common. Textbooks are selected by school boards of education, purchased according to schedules dictated by the academic year and assigned to users (students) regardless of those readers' own preferences. Trade books are chosen by readers themselves based on personal interests and whims, discovered by bookstore browsers, and have sales patterns based on economic trends, holiday shopping habits, and the vagaries of popular taste.

Thus textbook sales are slow, steady, predictable, and boring. Trade book sales are prone to boom and bust, with sudden bestsellers emerging unpredictably while seemingly promising titles often flop spectacularly.

If Hoffman and Bronson had been deeply knowledgeable about these differences in the book businesses, they might have been hesitant to leap from one into the other. But they knew very little about either book business, and the financial risk they were undertaking in trying to expand from textbooks into trade books wasn't very large. So they decided to give it a try and see what happened.

Norma Hoffman, Harry's wife, and Betty Shepherd, the wife of regional sales representative David Shepherd, were on the front lines of this experiment. "Norma and Betty got on the phone and started calling bookstores," Hoffman remembers. "Norma sold twelve books the first day. And from then on, we started selling books by phone."

From this tiny beginning, Ingram's telephone sales operation soon bloomed into an integral link to the world of book retailers—initially in and around Nashville, but soon across a growing swath of the eastern United States. Carol McElwain became the leader of this telephone shop. She directed its operations as well as other customer service activities for thirty years until her own retirement in 2015. And the culture of personal service, in which everyone in the organization is prepared to spend time helping customers, which Norma and Betty helped create and Carol nurtured, remains a core value of Ingram to this day.

As a careful businessman still feeling his way in the book business, Bronson didn't rush hastily into expanding the trade book operations. Martha's version of the early months under Hoffman has become part of company lore. In her telling, Hoffman had to persuade Bronson to let him stock about five hundred book titles for sale to bookstores—a number to which Bronson reluctantly agreed. But as trade sales steadily grew, so did the number of titles Hoffman wanted to stock, which called for repeated negotiations with Bronson—to get permission to carry a thousand titles, then fifteen hundred, and so on.

Over time, both Harry and Bronson came to realize that one crucial source of value for Ingram's customers was its large and ever-growing inventory of book titles. The bigger the inventory, the easier it was for Ingram to satisfy the unpredictable requests of its bookseller customers—and the less need for those booksellers to ever do business with another supplier. By 1998, Ingram's book warehouses were carrying 400,000 different book titles—a number that neither Hoffman nor Bronson could originally have imagined.*

* For historical information on the growth of Ingram's title base, see the appendix titled "Key Data on Ingram Growth" on page 214.

* * *

As Ingram's trade book sales began to grow, so did the company infrastructure dedicated to serving the new customer base. The warehouse staff increased, as did the number of people working in the burgeoning telephone sales department.

With Bronson's blessing, in 1970, Hoffman relocated the warehousing operations from downtown to a location closer to air and ground shippers on the city's less-congested southeastern fringe, near the Nashville airport. The new business address was 347 Reedwood Drive, since the street had been named in honor of the book depository's founder, Forest Reed. This location would become increasingly valuable in the years to come as Ingram's book distribution operations would grow explosively—first across the nation, then around the world. For a company in the distribution business, logistics are not a mere technical detail but a crucial element in the profit model, and one key to Ingram's long-term success would be the company's superlative management of logistical challenges.

Among Ingram Book Company's first executive hires during the Harry Hoffman era was Tom Clarkson. As he would be for many leaders in the early days of the company, Bronson was instrumental in bringing Clarkson to Hoffman's attention.

Clarkson had grown up in Franklin, Tennessee. His father, Tommy Clarkson Sr., opened a bookstore there in the 1960s called The Book and Hobby Shop, and Tom Jr. recalls his dad making occasional visits to the Ingram Book Company warehouse to pick up books for his store.

Clarkson had earned a degree in electrical engineering at Vanderbilt, then spent several years as a communications system engineer in the aerospace industry in Northern Virginia. Seeking a path more aligned with his skills, he returned to Vanderbilt for a master's program in engineering management. Bronson had endowed this program at the School of Engineering in honor of his father.

Actively supporting the program, Bronson used his connections in the Nashville business community to attract prominent leaders to offer seminars to the business school students—people like Franklin Jarman, CEO of General Shoe Company (later Genesco Inc.); Edward Nelson, CEO of Commerce Union Bank (now part of Bank of America); and Jack Stambaugh, who regaled the students with stories from his years in the Eisenhower administration. Clarkson attended these seminars, where he met Bronson, whom he found "very businesslike but very approachable."

Thanks to this Vanderbilt association, in July 1970, Bronson recommended Clarkson to Hoffman for a position at the book company. Hoffman hired him as director of systems engineering. As Clarkson says, "I became the only antenna engineer in the book warehouse. I had to learn business computing on the job."

What Clarkson found at the young Ingram Book Company was a data-management system that was typical of systems in use in small to midsize businesses in the 1960s. All business functions were punch-card based and highly manual. These systems had been perfectly adequate for managing the textbook depository and serving Ingram's small number of library accounts, but they were woefully inadequate for the trade book business and the first few bookstore accounts that Ingram had recently secured.

None of this was unusual for the time. A transition was underway nationwide from the older, card-based systems (so-called unit record equipment) to computers that were becoming affordable for businesses the size of Ingram Book Company. Ingram's approach to this transition was to partner with a computer service bureau next door. Ingram was to share processing time, using about one-third of an IBM 360 mainframe computer's entire capacity to run its book business. (By comparison, the computing power housed in the smartphone in your pocket today is significantly greater than that offered by the IBM 360.)

Another part of the arrangement was that the systems analyst at the service bureau would develop the necessary computer programs to support the growing book company. At this stage in the evolving computer industry, there was virtually no off-the-shelf business software; companies were on their own to develop the systems they needed.

Making the situation especially challenging, the systems analyst had a good understanding of standard warehouse operations, but no knowledge of the book business. At Ingram, there was limited knowledge of the trade book business and no understanding of computerized system development and operation.

Typical of new computer systems, there were design mistakes and coding errors in the software. Clarkson's first six months at Ingram, he recalls, were consumed with "learning how to troubleshoot the system, which at first was horribly full of bugs, getting that system to work."

The depth of trade book knowledge at Ingram began to grow with another important early addition to the team—Michael Zibart. Michael's father Alan owned and operated Zibart's, a popular bookstore in Nashville near the Vanderbilt campus. Michael and his sister Eve Zibart had worked in the family bookstore while in college. In this way, Michael got to know many of the publishers' reps who covered the retail territories of the middle South.

After his graduation from Vanderbilt, in 1969, Michael lived in California for a year, then returned home to Nashville. That's when, at his father's insistence, Michael visited Hoffman at the Ingram warehouse.

"I have a memory of my father taking me out to the book company and introducing me to Harry, and Harry talking to me," Zibart says. This led to a job offer, and Zibart joined the business in the fall of 1970. "The Christmas season was starting, and they were just gearing up to really do well. Frank Roberts was the buyer—I was, in theory, working for him—and he had bought all these books, and they didn't sell at all. When I first started working there, we had three million dollars' worth of dictionaries, as well as a lot of stuff we couldn't move."

Zibart was in the right place at the right time. He was able to suggest a simple solution to Ingram's overstock problem. Booksellers acquire their inventory from book publishers. So, of course, do book wholesalers like Ingram. And according to book industry custom dating back to the 1930s, books that don't sell at retail can go back to the publisher for full reimbursement. "I was the only one at Ingram who realized it," Zibart recalls. "Nobody at Ingram knew about returns. I got high on Harry's list then!"

Thanks in part to this bit of "inside knowledge" of the book business, Michael Zibart became Ingram's head buyer, managing relationships with the publishing companies that supplied the products Ingram was selling to its downstream customers. And at Hoffman's direction, Ingram Book soon developed its own procedures to add the management of book returns to its menu of services to retailers.

As the company grew, attracting more and more talented and hardworking people, Ingram's special corporate culture continued to take shape.

Patti Pigg—later Patti Freeman, after her marriage to another longtime Ingram associate—started at Ingram with a job in telephone sales. Having grown up in Franklin, Tennessee, and attended college and graduate school in Kentucky, she took a job at a Waldenbooks store in the RiverGate Mall just north of Nashville. But Pigg wasn't particularly happy working in a bookstore, and she began seeking other opportunities.

"It was 1976," she remembers. "I had a master's in English and couldn't find a job anywhere. A friend of mine who worked with me at Walden told me, 'Ingram is hiring, and they're really growing. You should go out there and talk to them.' So I went out to 347 Reedwood Drive and had a meeting with Mike Zibart."

When Zibart asked Pigg why she wanted to work at Ingram Book Company, she pointed to her degree in English. Zibart was unimpressed. "Well, that won't help you," he responded. "In fact, it might hurt you. And don't be wanting to work here because you like books, because that's not what we need."

Pigg was not deterred. "Whatever you need, I'll do it," she replied. It must have been the right answer, because Zibart hired her and put her to work. She began by helping manage the so-called fill list—manually tabulating the number of items filled compared to items out of stock on the green-bar printouts generated from telephone sales for the warehouse to pick, pack, and dispatch to waiting customers. This painstaking clerical work was tedious, but performing it accurately was vital to Ingram's reputation for good service.

"I did that for two weeks," Pigg recalls, "and I thought 'I can't stand this anymore.'" Fortunately for her, Ingram's rapid growth soon opened up a new opportunity for her as a buyer of mass-market paperback books—a job that gave her the chance to learn a lot about the publishing business and to expand her skill set.

Patti Pigg went on to have a varied career in and around the book business, as we'll detail later. But through it all, Pigg always looked back on her early years at Ingram as the happiest time of her career.

"I was stupid and just starting out," she now recalls with a laugh.

But we had so much fun! We were on the side of the angels. We believed that it was important for people to read books, and the fact that this was our mission made the work so meaningful. And the crazy ways we had to improvise to get the work done made it even better. It was so much fun when Harry would come over and announce, "Hey everybody—we're swamped with orders! Everybody over to the warehouse!" And then there were the times when Harry would get a bunch of people together and say, "Let's go sailing!" And we'd all go out on his boat and spend the day brainstorming business problems. Great ideas sprang from those days on the water.

Patti Pigg wasn't the only person who considered it fun to work at Ingram in its early days. In the seasons of heavy volume, especially the late fall just before the rush of holiday sales when booksellers would enjoy the bulk of their business for the year, everyone on the Ingram team would join in the work of picking orders for shipment. Zibart remembers, "'All hands on deck' meant all hands on deck. It didn't matter what your rank was."

To this day, longtime Ingram associates speak about how much they admire this aspect of the book company's culture. Sharon Hillman Fields was an Ingram associate from her college graduation until her retirement thirty-nine years later. She joined the company as a freight clerk in June 1976 and retired in 2015 as vice president and controller. She speaks of Ingram as "a family business" in two senses—its ownership and its culture of shared dedication.

> The seventies and eighties were a time of huge growth for the company, and that meant a lot of hard work. But even as a young person I could see that hard work and dedication were rewarded by the Ingram family. Working together to build a company brought all of us associates together as a family, building a strong bond that continues today. We were all just working together, no one more important than anyone else. And because we were all part of the team—feeling like owners just as much as the members of the Ingram family—we had a great feeling of accomplishment when we looked at the success of the company. Our blood ran "Ingram blue," you might say.

Bronson and the management team he assembled inspired this kind of commitment to go above and beyond the call of duty. As a result, Ingram Book Company was virtually always able to rise to the occasion—to satisfy the needs of its customers even when the volume and complexity of demands seemed overwhelming.

This get-it-done attitude—a combination of esprit de corps and creative thinking—was a major force behind the period of extraordinary success that Ingram would soon begin to experience.

4

THE FIRST BIG BREAKTHROUGH

By the early 1970s, Bronson Ingram and Harry Hoffman were becoming a powerfully effective leadership team for the Ingram Book Company. Bronson provided focus, strategic clarity, an instinctive understanding of the relationship between risk and reward, and a deep personal commitment to operational excellence—the last ingredient heightened by the sense of responsibility that comes with being an heir to a great family business. When necessary, Bronson could also provide the toughness needed to turn good intentions into effective action. Hoffman observed that firsthand. "I was one of the few people," Hoffman recalls, "that Bronson never really yelled at in all the time I was there."

For his part, Hoffman provided charisma and charm, a natural salesman's empathy for customers, and an innovative, opportunistic spirit. Together the ingredients provided by these two executives helped produce the first big bookselling innovation developed by Ingram: the information system made possible by the Ingram Microfiche Reader.

In these earliest days of the Ingram Book Company, it was becoming clear that the intermediary function could be a daunting, complicated task. Connecting publishers and their products with retail booksellers and their customers required the rapid but careful management of a vast volume of data, and the development of new tools and procedures that did not as yet exist. Sorting this out led to, in 1972, the launch of Ingram's microfiche revolution. To understand its significance, you need to know a little about the cumbersome, inefficient book distribution system that existed when the fledgling Ingram Book Company was first securing its foothold in the publishing business.

* * *

AT THAT TIME, THOUSANDS OF bookstores mostly ordered their stock directly from publishers, of which there were literally hundreds, including dozens of big ones. Because most orders were small and the convention was that the bookstores paid "the freight" (that is, the shipping costs), publishers shipped most of the stock the cheapest way, which was the postal service's fourth-class book rate. (This was a slow but very economical shipping method whose origins can be traced back to Benjamin Franklin and the other founders of our nation. Eager to make the postal service a tool for unifying, informing, and educating the far-flung population of the brand-new United States, they mandated that printed materials, including books, should be delivered at the lowest price possible. The arrangement persists today as the Media Mail service.)

Furthermore, the extremely decentralized and fragmented nature of the book market, with its hundreds of vendors and thousands of buyers, all operating independently, meant that each store had many small book orders to deal with all the time, with very uncertain delivery windows. And in those pre-computer days, just comparing deliveries to orders was daunting.

An efficient, unified system of nationwide book wholesalers could have simplified matters. But no such system existed in the early 1970s.

At that time, there were really just two kinds of book wholesalers. So-called library wholesalers enabled libraries to get any book they wanted from a single source. However, these were not really wholesalers as the term is used in almost every other industry, since libraries do not resell the books they purchase but rather make them available free to readers who visit their reading rooms or borrow them to read at home. The library wholesalers also offered few of the services that a true wholesaler in most industries provides. They stocked almost no inventory and banked on their customers' collective willingness to wait for fulfillment. And they sold books to their library customers at full price (unlike true wholesalers, which sell products to stores at a discount price, thereby enabling the stores to resell them and enjoy a profit margin of their own).

The leading library wholesaler, Baker & Taylor, had a small business serving bookstores as well, but their systems and personnel were geared to the needs of librarians rather than booksellers, so they were a minor factor in the business of trade publishing. (Ingram's modest library business in the early 1970s was competing against Baker & Taylor's much bigger operation.)

The other wholesalers were independent distributors of magazines and mass-market paperbacks, often called ID wholesalers. Mass-market paperbacks were small, inexpensive, cheaply produced books that represented yet another unique niche in the publishing business. They generally focused on unpretentious literary categories—mysteries, thrillers, romances, Westerns, and the like—and were sold originally on spinner racks in drugstores and other mass merchant outlets. After being on sale for a month or so, unsold mass-market paperbacks were stripped of their covers, which were returned for credit to the publisher, while the rest of the contents were pulped. Like magazines and newspapers, these mass-market books were treated as disposable items with a brief life span. In later years, from the late 1960s to the 1980s, mass-market paperbacks became a popular channel for reprinting and marketing trade book bestsellers originally published in hardcover.

By 1970, mass-market paperbacks had started to be sold in trade bookstores, rather than just in the traditional outlets. But the ID wholesalers were far from being major sources of books for bookstores. They stocked very few of the thousands of trade book titles; their focus was on a handful of bestsellers in hot demand at any given time.

Strictly speaking, Ingram Book Company was not comparable with either the library wholesalers or the ID wholesalers. But you can see from the description of these two types of wholesaler operations that neither offered booksellers much in the way of efficiency, service, or comprehensive availability. To run a bookstore, you had to accept the cumbersome reality of ordering from dozens if not hundreds of publishers and never really knowing when any particular shipment would arrive. The limited stock at the ID wholesalers would not cover even a tenth of what booksellers wished to offer. In much the same way, the Ingram Book Company itself suffered the problem that most of the books ordered from them were titles they didn't carry, no matter how fast they tried to increase their selection of books from the many, many publishers.

Under the circumstances, it's no wonder that book publishing—in particular the trade book business—was widely regarded as a chronically sick industry. Scholar and editor Jacques Barzun summed up the attitude of most observers in his 1957 essay "Paradoxes of Publishing":

> The phrase "marketing of books" is in itself a paradox, a rebuke to sanity. What marketing of books? Tradition and a faith in things not seen maintain the bookstore, which the trade calls an outlet; actually, it is a bottleneck, a plugged-up medicine dropper. The census reports some 2,900 bookstores, defined as stores doing more than half of their business in books. Greeting cards, novelties, records, knitting wool fill up the other half, so that publishers count only some 800 to 1,000 as "effective bookstores." The trade consoles itself with the axiom that the United States is "not a reading country." If hamburgers were as inaccessible as books, the United States would have to be put down as "not an eating country."

Leonard Shatzkin, whose study of the economics of book publishing we quoted earlier, offered further evidence of the difficulties readers experienced when seeking out books fully twenty-five years after Barzun's commentary:

Survey after survey confirms that half the people going into bookstores walk out disappointed. These surveys are almost invariably conducted along the stretch of Fifth Avenue in New York that houses the greatest concentration of titles available for sale in the English-speaking world. The ratio of disappointment is higher almost everywhere else, because there are even fewer books available. In the skimpily stocked stores that make up the majority of retail shops, the selection may be so limited that at least part of the potential clientele has learned not to bother coming in at all.

A book wholesaler like Ingram that hoped to improve this frustrating reality by applying the emerging technologies of the 1970s faced still other problems. Some were primarily technical and administrative. As described in chapter three, Ingram had partnered with a computer service bureau to convert its business systems from mostly manual to computer-supported processes. To accomplish this transition, it was necessary for Ingram to establish a unique identifying code for each book title handled. At that time, there were no universal book numbers in the publishing business. Instead, every publisher—from the giants like Random House and Simon & Schuster to small independent publishers— had its own internal coding system, no two of which were compatible.

Ingram's unique internal identifier was the five-digit title code inherited from Tennessee Book Company. Assigning the title code to the books on incoming orders from school systems was not a problem for Tennessee Book because of the small number of titles carried in that depository inventory. Matching the correct title code to each item in a wide range of titles on incoming orders from retail bookstores was another matter.

Order taking was a cumbersome manual process requiring Ingram employees to write the titles desired by booksellers on legal pads by hand. This was followed by a time-consuming search through inventory lists of one sort or another to find the correct title code for the book ordered, then writing it on the legal pad. Finally, the legal pads were sent to the keypunch section, where the orders were keyed into cards which could be read into the new computer system.

Not only was the process of identifying the correct title code for a book a major bottleneck to processing booksellers' orders, but also there was the broader problem of missing or inaccurate information from booksellers as well as the general book-buying public. In the absence of any universal product identifying codes or numbers, book orders were placed with title and author names, which weren't always correct. Then as now, it was not uncommon for two or more books to have identical or almost-identical titles. And bookstore workers, to say nothing of customers, would often misremember or garble the titles of books or authors they'd heard about in conversation or seen fleetingly mentioned in the local newspaper.

Tom Clarkson set about trying to get a handle on this chaos. Clarkson worked with internal colleagues and the staff of the computer service bureau to investigate different approaches that might improve the efficiency of associating the correct title code with titles on bookseller orders. Looking up the title codes on a microfilm inventory list was considered, but searching back and forth over a roll of microfilm was clumsy and impractical. The service bureau had designed a sophisticated computer program that identified the correct title code with an accuracy of over 99 percent. However, as the volume of Ingram's business grew, even this level of performance resulted in an unacceptable number of incorrect books being sent to customers.

On a trip to New York to visit publishers in 1970 or 1971, Hoffman learned that Random House had addressed its own internal organizational challenges with the technology called microfiche. In fact, he saw microfiche being used by an accountant at Random House.

Microfiche technology was far from brand-new at this point. The basic system, invented in 1961 by an engineer at the National Cash Register Company in Ohio, involved the microprinting of data onto a sheet of clear film. This so-called fiche could then be inserted by hand into a table-top projector that resembled a television set. A researcher would retrieve and read the information by moving a reading lens randomly over the sheet of film. It worked much like the conventional microfilm readers in a library, but the microfiche sheet was much handier to handle, ship, and read than the cumbersome spools of standard microfilm, and it also could be updated more easily and frequently.

Interestingly, microfiche had been widely commercialized by Hoffman's previous employer, Bell & Howell, though Hoffman himself would later say that he had not encountered it during his years with the company.

Hoffman was most impressed by the capacity of the compact microfiche sheets. "That's the thing that triggered me," he says, "when the fellow at Random House told me that each card could hold up to 20,000 items." The number was roughly equivalent to the number of book titles then in stock in the Ingram warehouse. Hoffman quickly surmised that using microfiche technology to maintain and update its inventory data could make it much easier for Ingram to do its internal coding. Title codes could be included with the book titles on a microfiche. Then a staff member could quickly look up the correct codes for the titles on order sheets. In addition, microfiche would replace internal paper catalogs used throughout the company, which were bulky as well as costly to update and print. The much smaller microfiche sheets, about four by six inches in size, could be updated and distributed weekly. That was the motivation for Hoffman to learn more.

"Let's get a sample in here," Clarkson remembers Hoffman saying, "and see if it would work for us."

They contacted Bell & Howell and requested a demonstration of the equipment. A sales rep followed up and scheduled a visit. However, when the salesman arrived, he brought lots of brochures with product information—but no machine. His explanation: the reader device would not fit into his Corvette sports car. Clarkson remembers the scene: "Harry's a salesman. Harry was unhappy. Shall we just say that?"

The salesman was excused from this scene of disappointment, and Hoffman returned to his desk. He picked up his desk phone and called his old boss in Chicago. "We want to see a microfiche reader. We may buy ten or twelve of these things, and your guy couldn't even bring a sample out here."

The next week, a national official of the vendor arrived at the Ingram office. The Ingram executives discussed with him their plan to use microfiche as an internal tool for coding book orders more efficiently. The official confirmed this was a feasible approach, and he discussed the details of what would be required to implement the plan.

The Bell & Howell representative's next statement transformed the proposed project into a much bigger one that would in fact end up revolutionizing the book business. The representative said, "Let me tell you what we're doing in the pharmaceutical business." He went on to say that Bell & Howell was already in the process of installing microfiche readers in local drugstores to make it easier for pharmacists to order supplies from their wholesalers. The concept was for pharmacists to look up the items they wanted to order along with the associated item codes using a catalog on microfiche. They would then order over the phone by giving the wholesaler the wholesaler's own codes. He suggested that it would be a logical step to apply the same approach to the book business.

The Ingram executives realized immediately that it would work. Ingram could provide each bookseller with a microfiche containing the book titles Ingram stocked along with the Ingram title codes. Then customers could look the title codes up themselves and order by the codes instead of by the (sometimes incorrect) titles. That would cut costs, errors, and delays, making life easier for everybody.

Both Clarkson and Michael Zibart—two Ingram managers who came from bookstore families—remember thinking that booksellers would find it a tremendous boon to know in advance of ordering what titles Ingram actually stocked. Remember, the stores were then living in a world where they had to send out book orders having no idea at all whether or when they would get the books. If every independent bookseller in the country could have access to an Ingram microfiche showing the titles currently held in the company's warehouse, the process of ordering and receiving books in the store could be made incalculably easier, faster, and more reliable.

The challenge for the bookstores, though, would be paying for the microfiche reader, which was not a cheap piece of hardware. Ingram decided to solve that problem by taking a subscription approach, including the machine and a weekly updated microfiche for ten dollars a month. Then they would turn around and charge the publishers a "listing fee" of one dollar a month per title for being on the microfiche. Those charges would finance the creation and distribution of the microfiche inventory data.

Of course, Ingram still had to convince booksellers that this new idea would really work. A sample of the proposed microfiche and a reader were obtained from Bell & Howell, and the concept was shown to local booksellers. Zibart and Clarkson gave their bookseller fathers demonstrations when they came to pick up orders for their stores. Both agreed on the spot to participate when the program was initiated.

Perhaps the most significant vote of confidence came when Hoffman tested the concept with Faith Brunson, the buyer at Rich's department store in Atlanta. (At that time, book departments in the big department stores were one of the major outlets of the book trade. Today, the department stores themselves are an endangered species, and their role in the book business is negligible.)

As Hoffman recalls, Brunson was skeptical at first. When told that the microfiche machine would cost her $120 in annual rent, she replied, "I would never pay you to buy books from you!" But she agreed to discuss the concept further in a nearby cafe. Over coffee, Hoffman spelled out all the advantages his microfiche system offered. By the time he was done, Brunson had changed her tune: "I'll pay anything for that machine," she declared.

"That was when I realized that we really had something that was going to be very important," Hoffman says. It may also have been one of the first times the leaders of Ingram recognized the principle that would be crucial to much of the company's future growth—taking advantage of Ingram's position as an intermediary in the book business to develop services that add value for its customers on both the upstream and the downstream sides of the supply chain.

* * *

DURING THE SUMMER OF 1973, Hoffman and Zibart demonstrated the reader in Los Angeles at the big national trade show of the American Booksellers Association, attended by tens of thousands of bookstore owners and buyers. After those first demonstrations, several hundred booksellers agreed to accept the machines. "That was the big coming-out party for the microfiche," Zibart says.

Bookstores could now place an order for a miscellaneous assortment of books from a range of publishers with the reasonable expectation that they would get just about every item on the list pretty quickly. The impact of this change was breathtaking. It was suddenly possible for stores to really manage their inventory. More and more of them turned to Ingram as a primary source because of that crucial benefit.

Further, the ability to order by Ingram title code yielded the anticipated benefits to both Ingram and booksellers. Phil Pfeffer, who would join Ingram in 1975, recalls how the company's burgeoning telephone sales operation benefited from this more efficient identification system: "Establishing the title codes to identify books, so you didn't have to read a long title and not be sure that you're talking about the same book, or the same edition, and whether it was a hardcover, a trade paperback, or a mass market paperback—this was just such a big improvement over the old way of doing things, and the market was very receptive to it."

Over time, booksellers even began to rely on Ingram's inventory as a virtual extension of their own. In the words of Kent Freeman, who later helped drive a further evolution of Ingram's information systems, "When a customer would ask a bookseller for a particular book, the bookseller would often say, 'If you don't find it on the store shelf, let me know. I'll check our warehouse and order you a copy.' But it was really Ingram's warehouse they were checking."

From Ingram's point of view, the benefits were equally great. Now almost all the orders they got were for titles they had and could supply. Going from a 10 percent fill rate to a 90 percent fill rate on the typical bookstore order produced off-the-charts growth in sales and profits. As a result, Ingram became a major national account for just about every publisher almost overnight. And within eighteen months, ten thousand book retailers around the United States had subscribed to the Ingram microfiche system.

Although the development of the microfiche program focused primarily on retail booksellers, libraries had many of the same needs, especially in regard to bestsellers and other new books. Thus a significant number of libraries also subscribed to the microfiche program.

Another result was a dramatic change in attitude among book publishers toward Ingram. In the beginning, publishers were mostly worried whether the fledgling book distributor from Tennessee could be trusted to pay its bills. By 1973, publishers were beginning to worry about staying on the good side of Ingram because Ingram was selling a lot of their books in a rapidly changing retail market.

Hoffman remembers, "When I first started visiting publishers and booksellers early in my time at Ingram, they didn't know me from Adam. But then I became a big deal. Ingram became a volume seller of books, and that made us important players on the industry stage."

In 1976, Baker & Taylor, the book wholesaler that competed with Ingram in serving the library market, introduced their own version of the microfiche system for bookstores. However, B&T didn't have the breadth of stock that Ingram did, nor the speed of delivery, and their systems were not as robust or accurate. Thus, at that time they failed to mount a true challenge to Ingram as the wholesaler of choice for independent bookstores. However, the advent of microfiche at both Ingram and B&T meant that the entire book supply chain had become dramatically more efficient. This would make it possible in the years to come for both independent and chain bookstores to grow very quickly in number and title selection.

The microfiche revolution was also part of a larger process of rationalization in the handling of book industry data. The streamlining and unification of title identification systems across the publishing business was hastened by the subsequent adoption of the modern International Standard Book Number, or ISBN, system. Originated by the British book retailer W. H. Smith and a committee of UK publishers in 1965, the ISBN system was officially adopted as a worldwide standard by the International Organization for Standardization (ISO) in 1970. It was gradually accepted by American publishers, distributors, and retailers during the 1970s, and by the mid-1980s the printing of a bar code containing the ten-digit ISBN number on a book's cover had become ordinary practice among US publishers. A thirteen-digit ISBN became standard on January 1, 2007.

Over time, Ingram's microfiche system evolved to become even more valuable to booksellers and libraries. For example, Ingram personnel noticed that booksellers would often call to place orders based on publicity and marketing events related to a particular book—even without having author or title information. A bookstore clerk might call Ingram and say, "We've had four requests this week for that book they talked about on *The Today Show* on Monday. Sorry, I'm not sure about the title or the author's name."

You can imagine how frustrating this was for the Ingram salespeople. It was asking too much to expect them to personally research every query of this kind. Even if they had the time to call *The Today Show*, their queries would often go unanswered; after all, responding to a question from a clerk working for a book wholesaler in Tennessee was not usually a top priority for a TV producer at the NBC studios in New York.

The Ingram team realized that their system for capturing and tracking book information might have the potential to fix this problem. Clarkson and his team altered the programming of their microfiche records to include a space for marketing information—author tour events, major book reviews, TV interviews, and the like. Then they began asking publishers to provide information to fill this slot on the card—which meant that a quick scan of the latest microfiche records would enable any Ingram employee to identify the mystery book that had been featured on *The Today Show* on a given date and dispatch several copies to a store.

As publishers realized the value of this marketing feature, they made certain that information of future events was always sent to Ingram. Being able to read these advance notices on the microfiche meant stores could have titles in stock before the events promoting them occurred.

As you can imagine, this made the booksellers as well as the publishers happy, and gave them a new ability to turn big publicity breaks into real book sales. It also drastically reduced the frustration level of authors who'd long suffered when their hard-won efforts to get media attention for their books proved fruitless because of the book business's inefficient data pipeline.

Appreciative of the important role Clarkson had played in making Ingram a leader in bookselling technology, Hoffman would later make Clarkson the company's vice president for information technology. After his departure from Ingram in 1982, Clarkson spent nine years consulting for large book retailers, including the technical staff of Waldenbooks, then a leading national bookstore chain. He completed his career at Barnes & Noble booksellers in New York City. He continued to participate in the industry-wide technical consortium called the Book Industry Study Group, for which he had been the Ingram company representative. Over the years, BISG has helped drive further technological and systems innovations that have benefited the entire book business.

Microfiche wasn't the only tool Ingram employed in its new role as a central information clearinghouse for the book publishing business. Ingram also began publishing monthly newsletters highlighting for booksellers all of the important new book titles being issued by the major publishers. Three separate newsletters were published: one for hardcover books, one for trade paperbacks, and one for mass-market paperbacks. Having news about books coming from all the publishers in a single source was extremely handy for booksellers, and Ingram's newsletters quickly became standard tools for the entire industry.

The microfiche reader would become one of the first examples of the unique role Ingram was able to play in modernizing the publishing business. As the leader of a large business enterprise with a track record of success in capital-intensive industries like oil production and barges, Bronson understood how to invest wisely in equipment and processes targeted to increase operational efficiencies. This was a managerial skill that was desperately needed in the highly decentralized book business, with its huge number of mostly small participants—publishing houses, bookstores, libraries—who lacked managerial expertise, were generally short on capital, and often operated on a hand-to-mouth basis. In coming up with the idea of the microfiche system for managing inventory efficiently, then making the system and the necessary tools available at a modest cost to thousands of small enterprises around the country, the Ingram Book Company single-handedly helped lift the book business into the twentieth century.

It was an impressive beginning—but only a beginning.

PART TWO
The Acceleration

5
A National Footprint

As Bronson Ingram, Harry Hoffman, and the rest of the Ingram team were growing their system—building their ability to simplify and streamline the process of book distribution—there was another company trying to pursue some of the same goals. This was Raymar Book Company, based in Pasadena, California.

Fran Howell and Stu Woodruff had founded Raymar in the early 1960s, naming it after their wives, Raymonde and Margaret. Woodruff had been a salesman for the Doubleday publishing house, and his years of working with booksellers had helped him understand how frustrating the traditional book distribution system was for them.

In some ways, Raymar could be considered the first true book wholesaler—a predecessor of what Ingram Book Company would ultimately become. Unlike the library wholesalers and the ID book-and-magazine distributors we described in chapter four, whose customer base and product selection were both rather limited, Raymar served the book trade with a wide array of general titles, both hardcover and paperback, from all the major publishers and many minor ones.

Raymar filled an especially important niche for booksellers in the West. The book publishing business was then (and still is today) largely centered on the East Coast, particularly in New York. Most books were physically produced at printing and binding facilities in the East, and most publishers maintained warehouses only in the East. So when a bookstore in California, Colorado, or Washington State ordered books from a publisher, they would often have to wait a few weeks for them to arrive. (Remember the cheap-but-slow fourth-class book rate that publishers relied on.) By the time the books turned up in the store, any potentially interested customers were likely to have forgotten all about them.

Raymar helped solve this problem. They had distribution centers in Southern California and the Seattle area, in which a large assortment of books from all the leading publishers were kept on hand. Nearby booksellers would actually visit these vast warehouses and shop firsthand for books with which to stock their own store shelves. Of course, they could also order books by phone for shipment to their stores by mail, and the products would arrive far more quickly than they would have if shipped from the East Coast.

By the mid-1970s, Howell and Woodruff had been engaged in book wholesaling for a dozen years. They and their company had built a strong, positive reputation in this field, including unmatched contacts and relationships in the region they served. And as Raymar grew, they began to hear more and more about a Nashville-based rival called Ingram, which was growing even more quickly.

One of Raymar's early hires was Art Carson, who joined the company in 1963 when he was just eighteen years old. From there, he had developed a broad understanding of the West Coast bookselling scene. Carson recalls what happened in the mid-1970s:

> Both Raymar and Ingram Book were growing rapidly at this time. At this point, Raymar chose to open a distribution center in Mundelein, Illinois, to serve the Midwest. I was sent out there to do the buying. But I believe the Raymar folks underestimated how well Ingram had grown to serve Midwestern booksellers. We found our sales didn't keep pace with the expense of running the distribution center. So after four years of trying to make a go of it, the owners closed the facility and brought me back to Southern California.

Raymar's failed attempt to establish a Midwestern foothold reflected not only Ingram's growing clout in the region but also Raymar's own thin capitalization. Unlike Ingram Book Company, Raymar was not part of a large business conglomerate with financial resources from other industries. The company's owners were continually stretched for cash, making it almost impossible for them to invest as needed to support the growth of the business.

Such financial difficulties were common among the small ranks of book wholesaling companies. In fact, as late as 1982, Leonard Shatzkin would write, "The peculiarities of book publishing make it extremely doubtful that wholesaling (despite the outstanding performance of one company, Ingram) can achieve stability and decent financial returns." The financial struggles of Raymar, despite the skill and experience of its owners, were evidence for Shatzkin's observation.

As time passed, Raymar and Ingram crossed paths increasingly often. "The two of us didn't directly compete for business except on rare occasions," Carson recalls, "though we did compete for inventory from publishers fairly often. In general, we thought of Ingram Book Company as friendly competitors. And of course we liked them personally. It was pretty much impossible to not be impressed and charmed by Harry Hoffman and his wife Norma."

Eventually, the idea of Ingram buying Raymar as a way of accelerating its own national expansion became increasingly obvious. Carson observes:

> Once Harry and Bronson decided they wanted to go national, acquiring Raymar, with its Southern California and Northwest distribution centers, made a lot of sense. It would instantly make Ingram into a national wholesaler. It also made sense for the Raymar owners, who were constantly facing money issues. Selling to the well-funded Ingram would ensure a better future for their associates.

Margaret Howell, whose husband Fran had cofounded Raymar, remembers it this way: "It was obvious to both Fran and Stu Woodruff that they either had to join Ingram or fight them. And they felt that they would be better off joining them and helping them be successful. And so that's how the getting together happened."

The Raymar acquisition in 1976 was a great leap forward for Ingram in several ways. It marked the serious beginning of Ingram's network of strategically placed distribution centers, each positioned near a regional population cluster across the continent. In 1974, Ingram had opened a second book warehouse and shipping center in Jessup, Maryland. Now Raymar's Pasadena and Seattle warehouses were added to the growing Ingram network. Then, in 1985, Ingram moved its original distribution center from its Reedwood Drive location near the Nashville airport into a larger facility in the town of La Vergne, Tennessee, twenty miles further southeast, where interstate highway I-24 crosses into Rutherford County. Building this nationwide distribution network was a key step in the development of the powerful logistical system that would produce benefits both for Ingram and for all its customers, from publishers to booksellers and beyond.

The Raymar acquisition also brought a number of talented, knowledgeable book people into the company. Art Carson became Ingram's director of marketing, and Fran Howell became the company's vice president of product purchasing. Howell's partner at Raymar, Stu Woodruff, was several years older, and he chose to retire rather than join the Ingram team.

* * *

LIKE MOST COMPANY ACQUISITIONS, INGRAM'S purchase of Raymar was not without its complications. There was a relatively minor problem related to the organization of the Raymar distribution centers, which doubled as sales outlets for local booksellers who would visit them to stock up on titles they needed to fill their own store shelves. In the Raymar centers, books were stocked and displayed according to publisher—all the Random House books on one set of shelves, all the Simon & Schuster books on another, and so on. For booksellers accustomed to thinking about books as products made and sold by individual publishers, this was a logical system that made it easy for them to find specific books they wanted.

Therefore, when Ingram's own inventory management systems were implemented at Raymar's facilities—including shelving the books according to Ingram's own numbered system rather than by publisher—the local booksellers had to adjust to a new way of finding the books they wanted. Soon, the custom of allowing booksellers to browse Ingram's warehouses was abandoned altogether, disrupting the retailers' habits even further.

Fortunately, Ingram offered other advantages that Raymar couldn't match, including a larger number of book titles in stock. In relatively short order, these benefits helped booksellers accept the new arrangements.

Somewhat more complicated were the financial challenges that Ingram had to tackle as a result of the Raymar acquisition. These were among the first big tasks facing Philip M. Pfeffer, an executive who would go on to be one of the most important leaders in Ingram's history.

Pfeffer and his wife Pam had moved to Nashville in 1966, shortly after both graduated from Southern Illinois University at Carbondale, so Phil could do his graduate work in economics at Vanderbilt University. In January 1968, with his doctoral degree nearly completed, Pfeffer joined Genesco as an economist in the company's executive training program. He was soon promoted to manager of Genesco's international finances. By this time, Genesco was beginning to acquire new apparel manufacturing capabilities outside the United States, principally in Europe. Founded in 1924, Genesco's holdings eventually included the New York City retailer Bonwit Teller and the S. H. Kress & Co. retail chain.

Pfeffer's work at Genesco involved dealing with the United States government's Office of Foreign Direct Investment and navigating a new set of financial rules imposed by the Johnson administration on international currency transactions. The new rules limited the use of US-sourced funding for overseas acquisitions. For Genesco, this meant establishing a facility to sell debt denominated in US currency but funded outside the United States.

"We did one of the first euro-dollar bond issues," Pfeffer recalls. "One way we established interest rates was the London Interbank Overnight Rate. That's where LIBOR came from—one of the most influential determinants of global interest rates—and our company was deeply involved in helping to shape these early markets."

Pfeffer's rise at Genesco soon accelerated. He was named president of the company's exports and military sales business. (By this time, Genesco was producing uniforms, footwear, and fatigues for the US troops serving in Vietnam.) He was promoted to assistant treasurer of Genesco Inc., the parent company, with responsibility for the company's cash management activities and banking relationships.

Because of Genesco's prominence in Nashville business circles, Pfeffer was invited to join the Financial Executives Institute (later called Financial Executives International), an elite international organization. There he met George Kaludis, president of FEI's Nashville chapter, who had previously been the vice chancellor for finance and administration at Vanderbilt. Then he'd left the university to join Ingram Book Company as an executive vice president reporting to Hoffman.

"One night after an FEI meeting," Pfeffer recalls, "George was telling me about Ingram Book Company, where he was now working, and how much opportunity he saw there. He described their interest in creating a position to help the company better finance its business through the management of its cash flow, and he asked me whether I might be interested."

After a successful interview with Bronson, Pfeffer was offered the job. He became Ingram's director of financial planning, reporting to Kaludis. And that's why, in 1976, the job of sorting out Raymar's complex financial problems fell into his lap.

Both Raymar's receivables and its payables, it turned out, were a mess. "This can happen to book distributors," Pfeffer recalls.

> If they don't manage their receivables with their customers—the bookstores—a wholesaler can get in trouble fast. Even though publishers have historically given fairly generous payment terms, if the level of debt owed by the booksellers becomes too great, then the wholesaler may be unable to pay the publishers when the cost of books purchased becomes due. Then the tendency is to pay whichever publisher complains the loudest, rather than paying everybody on the same terms—for example, setting up a consistent plan to pay everyone within forty-five days. When you get into the habit of juggling payments, you create a lot of uncertainty and ill-will with your suppliers.

That was the dilemma that Raymar was in. And when Ingram acquired Raymar, it assumed the company's liabilities, which were a lot worse than anyone had realized.

As director of financial planning, my job was to turn the cash flow of the business around. And they gave me a tremendous amount of latitude—George did, Harry did. They let me do whatever needed to be done. At the time, Ingram Book Company was a very small investment of Ingram Corporation. The corporation's money and the focus of the top executives was on other businesses. So it was up to me to solve this cash flow problem.

Fortunately, Ingram had a couple of big things working in its favor. One was the nature of bookseller financing. Bookstores bought their inventory from two main sources—directly from individual publishers and from wholesalers who distributed books from a wide range of publishers. Raymar, and now Ingram, were the industry's two leading trade wholesalers. Now, if a bookseller was experiencing financial problems, it would typically choose to pay its debts to the wholesalers prior to paying off the individual publishers. The reason is obvious: The wholesalers would play a more central role in a bookseller's daily operations, since it was to the wholesalers that the booksellers would turn whenever they needed to replenish their inventory. (They would buy direct from publishers much more infrequently—perhaps twice a year, when the fall or spring titles were issued by the publishing houses.) So when Pfeffer and his team, having taken over Raymar on behalf of Ingram, began contacting the booksellers about the money they owed, they were generally able to collect on the debt without a lot of difficulty.

The second big advantage Ingram enjoyed was the skyrocketing sales revenues they'd begun to experience ever since introducing the microfiche inventory management system. The efficiency, speed, and accuracy of that system had made Ingram the overwhelming favorite source of book supplies among booksellers. As a result, Ingram's sales had begun a steep ascent. By 1977, Ingram Book Company's annual revenues had reached $36 million. In the years that followed, sales volume continued to expand at a rapid pace.[1]

These advantages helped Phil Pfeffer and his financial team resolve the problem of the outstanding debt held by Raymar. It took about a year and a half to get the tangled cash flow challenges sorted out. After this, for the

[1] For historical information on Ingram's revenue growth, see the appendix titled "Key Data on Ingram Growth" at the end of this book.

first time, Ingram's trade book business—as opposed to the textbook and library business operated through the Tennessee Book Company—became consistently profitable.

It was an important turning point, ensuring there were no major financial obstacles to further growth for Ingram. In the years to come, Ingram's leaders would work hard to make sound financial stewardship a hallmark of the company's operations. This provided a solid base from which to engage in increasingly creative and imaginative business experiments, especially in the use of technology to provide value-adding services to Ingram's customers. Executives constantly preoccupied with managing a heavy debt load can't afford to take chances on such experiments, even ones with enormous growth potential. Ingram's leaders could.

* * *

INGRAM'S NEW POSITION AS THE leading national book wholesaler might have led the company to become complacent. But that doesn't seem to be part of the Ingram DNA. The stream of process and system improvements coming from Ingram to benefit its customers continued. One example: the introduction of shrink-wrapping as a standard packaging process in book wholesaling.

"Historically," Pfeffer recalls, "bookstores would complain about damaged dust jackets, crinkled paperback covers, dented book covers, and other flaws that made the products we'd shipped them hard to sell. Shrink wrap was the solution. We started shrink-wrapping each book carton and sending it through a heat machine that would produce a tight, secure package to go to the bookstore. The complaints about damaged books pretty much went away after that. It was Ingram that introduced shrink wrap to the book industry."

Meanwhile, Ingram's marketing team was developing further innovations. One of these was a service for new bookstore owners that came to be called Recommended Opening Store Inventory (ROSI). ROSI enabled new booksellers to launch their businesses more quickly and efficiently by recommending choices for their initial title stocking decisions based on Ingram research geared to store size, sales experience in the region, and other factors. Ingram had this information in abundance.

The need for ROSI was driven by a nationwide trend—the opening of shopping malls, separate from traditional downtown retailing districts, in response to the explosion of suburban communities around the United States.

Shopping malls anchored by large department stores and equipped with vast parking areas had begun to proliferate in post-war America. Business historians often cite the Southdale Center in Edina, Minnesota, as the first modern shopping mall. Opened in 1956, it was fully enclosed and had a two-level design, with comfortable common areas featuring central air conditioning and heating. By 1964, there were some 7,600 malls around the United States. By 1972, that number had almost doubled, to more than thirteen thousand, and during the remainder of the decade and into the 1980s the number of malls continued to explode. A variety of new mall formats were created, including so-called vertical malls in urban neighborhoods, beginning with Water Tower Place on Michigan Avenue in Chicago, and super-regional centers larger than 800,000 square feet.

The mall explosion led to the opening of thousands of new stores in every category, from apparel to home furnishings, appliances to electronic equipment. Bookstores became part of this trend. A number of bookstore chains were launched during the '60s and '70s, and soon became familiar features in malls around the country. They included:

- *Waldenbooks.* The first Walden bookstore was opened in Pittsburgh in 1962 by a former Simon & Schuster salesman named Lawrence Hoyt; by 1977, under the name of Waldenbooks, the chain had expanded to 250 locations around the country.
- *B. Dalton.* In 1966, Bruce Dayton, a member of the Dayton family, which ran a department store chain out of Minneapolis, opened the first B. Dalton bookstore in Edina, Minnesota. By 1973, there were 125 B. Dalton stores scattered across the United States. Dalton were the first booksellers to make extensive use of inventory control data from across its entire store chain. This was made possible through the creation of unique SKU numbers for book titles (comparable to Ingram's introduction of its own unique identifying numbers) and a system of affixing each book with a special Dalton sticker. This cumbersome extra step became needless in the 1980s as ISBN numbers and bar codes were universally applied to book covers.
- *Barnes & Noble.* In 1971, an ambitious young bookseller named Len Riggio purchased the venerable Barnes & Noble book publishing and retailing business based in New York. By 1979, through acquisitions of smaller bookstore chains and the opening of numerous campus-based bookstores, B&N had become yet another rapidly expanding bookstore presence in communities around the country.

The opening of hundreds of new bookstores represented a significant strategic opportunity for a book wholesaler like Ingram. These new booksellers needed help in making sense of the complex and inefficient system for getting books into the hands of readers that had evolved over the decades. At the other end of the supply chain, the publishers were ill-positioned to provide this help, given the highly fragmented nature of the industry. As publishing expert and author Leonard Shatzkin observed:

> Each publisher commands such a small percentage of the total retail sales that a general increase in retailing effectiveness is likely to return him very little in absolute dollars. Since even a fairly substantial publisher is likely to get only 2 or 3 percent of the volume represented by a new store, he has very little reason to involve himself in either effort or money to help such a bookstore get started.

Recognizing this void, Ingram's marketing team set about developing innovative ways to serve the burgeoning new bookstore market, with the goal of making Ingram not just a supplier of products but an integral part of the bookselling process.

Patti Pigg, by this time a junior staffer in Ingram's marketing office, was part of the team designing the ROSI program to help retailers with little or no knowledge about bookselling enter the field. (As we mentioned earlier, Pigg had worked at a Walden bookstore before joining Ingram, so she had some firsthand understanding of the challenges of running a retail bookstore.) Most bookstores at that time were run on a rudimentary business basis. "They had no real inventory management systems," Pigg says, "just a card stuck in each book. And a lot of the stores didn't even have a cash register—just a cigar box to collect the money. They were run by people like me—English majors who loved books but didn't really know anything about business. That's why they needed Ingram's help."

Pigg's boss at the time was a woman named Dale Ziglar, whom Pigg recalls as being very much in the same mold as Hoffman—energetic, imaginative, optimistic, and innovative. "When other people at the company got nervous about a new idea, Dale would respond, 'Well, try it!' And a lot of the time, it worked!" Among other innovations, Ziglar had been the person to propose the monthly newsletters offering advance information about upcoming books from all the major publishers.

One of the major national retailers that was growing enormously in the mid-1970s was Kmart. Launched under the name of S. S. Kresge, Kmart had started with five-and-dime stores in Memphis (1897) and Detroit (1898). By 1962, the chain boasted several hundred discount stores. It then adopted the Kmart brand name and, within a few years, had grown into the nation's second-largest retailer, surpassed only by Sears.

The idea of expanding the chain's product offerings to include books was an obvious one. So when Ziglar suggested in a meeting, "What if we were to approach a company like Kmart and propose putting a book department in a Kmart store?" the concept resonated internally. And initial inquiries with Kmart revealed that the company had already begun thinking about the possibility.

Ziglar asked Pigg to go talk to Kmart about what Ingram could do for them. "We felt our service would be a good fit for Kmart," Pigg recalls. "They were smart, experienced retailers. But they didn't know anything about the book business. Our idea was, 'We'll design a complete book department for you. We'll train your people, we'll manage your inventory, we'll tweak the plans to match the neighborhood, we'll design the fixtures, and we'll even organize a grand opening event for you.'"

Among the many advantages of the Ingram store opening system was that it eliminated the need for store personnel to open cartons from dozens of different publishers, sort the books by category and subject area, and figure out how to shelve them appropriately. Instead, books from all publishers would be shipped from an Ingram warehouse to the new bookstore, already sorted by category and subject. Bookstore workers—many of whom might be working with books for the very first time—could simply open the cartons and put the books on the shelves.

Pigg arranged a meeting with Jim Gates, Kmart's chief merchandising officer. It was a big assignment, with both risk and opportunity riding on her presentation. "I went up there by myself to Kmart's office in Troy, Michigan," she recalls. "I was maybe twenty-five years old, and I looked even younger."

Gates was a traditional male executive who had worked his way up through the hierarchy of the Kresge chain. Pigg remembers his gruff demeanor, resembling the actor Ed Asner playing the hard-boiled newspaperman Lou Grant, complete with rolled-up shirtsleeves and a pencil tucked behind his ear. She remembers that when she entered his office, Gates didn't bother to stand up to greet her—in fact, he barely glanced in her direction.

"Hello, Mr. Gates," Pigg said. "I'm Patti Pigg, with Ingram Book Company."

Gates's response was dismissive: "You're not important enough to meet with me."

"Well, I'm the one that's here," Pigg replied.

"Are you a vice president?" Gates demanded.

"No, I'm not."

"Well, they should have at least sent a vice president to deal with me."

Thinking fast, she responded, "I'll tell you what we'll do. Let's call my boss. My boss is a vice president."

"What's your boss's name?"

"My boss's name is Dale Ziglar."

"And he's a vice president?"

Careful to avoid using either a male or female pronoun, Pigg replied, "Dale Ziglar is vice president of marketing of Ingram Book Company, yes. Let's get Dale on the phone!"

Gates shoved his desk phone toward her. With the speaker on, she dialed the number of the office on Reedwood Drive. In a moment, the phone was answered by Ziglar's assistant, Laura Brown.

"Hey, Laura, it's Patti. I'm with Mr. Gates here at Kmart. He has a question for Dale."

"Sure, just hold on a moment," Brown replied.

In a few seconds, Dale Ziglar spoke: "Hello?"

Puzzled by the feminine voice, Gates replied, "Uh, yes, Jim Gates here. We're holding for Dale Ziglar."

"This is Dale!" Ziglar declared.

Pigg smiles as she recalls Gates's reaction. "His eyes got real big," she says. "He was disturbed and befuddled. And Dale said, 'What can I do for you, Jim? Is Patti up there?'"

Gates finally replied, "Well, yes, she's here. But I'm just a little startled, if you want to do business with this big corporation, that you sent somebody like her to meet with me."

Ziglar was ready with a reply. "Well, Jim, I'll tell you what," she said. "Yes, it's true that Kmart is a big company. You're a lot bigger than Ingram Book Company is, and we know that. And we appreciate the opportunity to do business with you. And if you want to do business with us, you'll deal with the person that's sitting right there in front of you. And I'll tell you something else: Patti is our expert. She knows more about bookselling than most anyone else you can hope to meet. And if you're smart, you'll learn from her."

After a long pause, Gates finally responded. "Well, I guess I'll give her a chance."

Pigg explained to Gates how Ingram could support Kmart in the mission of opening new book departments in its stores around the country. She won Gates's confidence. "We worked with Kmart to design hundreds of book departments in 1977 and 1978," she remembers. "We did everything for them, from selecting books to designing shelving. And in the process, we learned a lot about inventory management, and about how we could help booksellers run their businesses more efficiently and profitably."

This was knowledge that would prove enormously valuable during the 1980s and 1990s, as the bookstore boom continued and morphed into new forms, providing tremendous opportunities for Ingram to play an expanding leadership role in a fast-growing industry. And the relationship between Pigg and Gates quickly grew past its rocky beginning. In fact, she fondly recalls the time he sent her flowers in gratitude for the help she'd provided—a far cry from the disdain he exhibited when they first met.

(In 1979, Pigg left Tennessee for Atlanta to work for Software Sciences, the maker of one of the inventory control systems that Ingram offered to bookstores. Fifteen years later, she joined Digital Equipment Corp. and later on IBM, NeXT, Apple, and Oracle—until her career brought her back to Ingram. In 2002, she ended up marrying Kent Freeman, a computer whiz whose contributions to Ingram's history of technological innovations we'll describe later in this book.)

Kmart's interest in the book business turned into a long-term relationship. Several years later, in 1984, Kmart bought the Waldenbooks chain. Then, in 1992, Kmart bought the smaller, upscale Borders bookstore chain and merged the two booksellers into the Borders-Walden Group. By that time, the business of bookselling was undergoing further change, particularly with the rise of book superstores—a topic we'll delve into more deeply in a later chapter.

6

HARRY HOFFMAN'S LEGACY

Within a few years of his arrival, Harry Hoffman had become the public face of Ingram Book Company. He had been the innovator, the captain, and the motivator of the growing team through its earliest years of wholesaling to the commercial book trade. He and Mike Zibart, by now Ingram's lead buyer, were the company's most visible ambassadors to the New York publishers and other industry leaders across Ingram's rapidly widening world.

One of the places where the Ingram Book Company made its growing presence felt in the United States publishing business was at the annual trade show then known as the American Booksellers Association (ABA) convention. Held the last weekend in May, usually in either New York, Chicago, or Los Angeles, the ABA was a grand affair, bringing together thousands of people from every corner of the book business: booksellers, publishers, editors, authors, literary agents, librarians, publicists, marketers, and many avid readers. (Since 1995, the ABA convention has been called BookExpo America.)

Lavish parties hosted by companies eager to promote their importance in the industry were part of the ABA program. Patti Pigg remembers attending the 1979 meeting in Atlanta, where the Omni Hotel's impressive open-air atrium was transformed into a festive party space with a huge hot air balloon as the decorative centerpiece. "And when the ABA was in New York," she recalls, "the number of celebrity authors in attendance would be phenomenal. You could be walking along the aisles of the convention floor and spot John Gregory Dunne and Joan Didion and Truman Capote strolling through. As an English major, these were my heroes!" Countless other people from the world of publishing felt the same way about the annual ABA event.

ABA also became a venue where Ingram forged and nurtured personal connections with people from every corner of the industry. This began in earnest in the company's first decade, when Hoffman and Zibart first took the Ingram Microfiche Reader prototype to the convention in order to pitch booksellers on its merits.

Over the years, Ingram became a fixture at ABA as well as the trade show's largest non-publishing exhibitor. Adorned with the company's royal blue logo, the Ingram "booth"—actually an enormous display area, some years as big as five thousand square feet—was where executives and sales associates greeted thousands of booksellers and small publishers from across the nation, and where new deals were made.

Much of Ingram's floor space inside the ABA booth would be devoted to replicating a model bookstore. The carpeted, walk-through Ingram Bookstore presented, on current-model shelving, displays of hardcover books in colorful dust jackets, magazines offered by Ingram Periodicals (a new division we'll describe later), and other materials describing Ingram's growing array of services. Judy Allen, the coordinator of all Ingram trade-show logistics, explains that the Ingram Bookstore display was originally codesigned by Ingram marketing professionals together with experts from Franklin Fixtures, the fabricator of the modern display shelving. (The booth also became the spot where both Franklin and Ingram would refer each other to interested booksellers who inquired.)

Ingram also became a prominent presence at the world's largest international trade shows, the London Book Fair and the Frankfurt Book Fair. These trade shows and their associated receptions on the periphery continue to be standard features on the book publishing calendar each year. Ingram family members and associates continue to attend them. These conventions and the many social events built around them regularly yield new business, new customers, new relationships, and often durable memories.

In the earliest years, members of the Ingram family didn't personally attend ABA. Phil Pfeffer eventually approached Bronson Ingram and his wife Martha and urged them to attend. Pfeffer recalls one of the booksellers, after meeting Bronson in the Ingram booth, exclaimed with surprise, "I never knew there was a Mr. Ingram! If it wasn't for you, I wouldn't be in the bookstore business."

"Bronson and Martha ate it up," Pfeffer says.

Soon Martha became a vivid presence at ABA, especially at the annual party for booksellers and publishers hosted by Ingram. Many people still recall the time she donned an apron and served chili at a Texas-themed Ingram party.

Things occasionally got rather raucous at the gatherings held in the orbit of ABA. Morgan Entrekin, a veteran publisher who now runs Grove/Atlantic, remembers a 1991 party his company threw for ABA attendees in Anaheim. Entrekin is a native of Nashville, where he had known the Ingram family for many years.

"I gave a big cocktail party, and I invited Bronson and Martha, along with a couple of hundred other people," Entrekin recalls.

> There was a literary agent who showed up intoxicated, and he and another agent got into a confrontation. One of the agents slugged the

other and flattened him. I rushed over to try to take control of the situation, and right then I saw Bronson and Martha entering the room close to where this fistfight had broken out.

I called out, "Hi, Bronson! Hi, Martha!" But they just waved, turned around, and left. I didn't blame them—who wants to walk into the middle of a fistfight? But it was pretty embarrassing for me.

Later I wrote Bronson a note, saying, "Thanks for coming to my party. Sorry a fistfight broke out."

Bronson replied, "Don't worry about it, Morgan. We're from Tennessee. What's a party without a good fistfight?"

I was always grateful to him for that response.

However, in the early years, before the Ingram family became an ABA fixture, it was Hoffman who dominated Ingram's presence at the convention. He became a widely recognized symbol of the company's innovative, collaborative, and all-embracing spirit. He spent long days strolling the convention floor and greeting visitors to the Ingram booth—book publishers, bookstore owners and managers, editors, literary agents, authors, and more. Harry was so closely linked with Ingram in the eyes of the publishing world that, when he left the company, Pfeffer said to his colleagues, "What we're going to need is a big, stand-up Harry doll to bring to trade shows."

Inside the company, too, Hoffman was a larger-than-life, motivating personality. Associates who remember those early days of the book company describe it as an exciting, innovative, and enjoyable place to work, and many credit Hoffman as the leader who helped make it so.

Johnny Secrest joined Ingram in 1976, starting out during his student days as a part-time and summer employee in the warehouse. Initially, he was attracted by Ingram's generous tuition reimbursement policies. Later, he realized it would be a great place to build a career. Secrest would spend decades at Ingram, eventually rising to the position of the company's chief logistics officer and overseeing the vast distribution system that had grown up around him during his years with the company.

He recalls his first glimpse of Hoffman early one morning before most of the other staffers had arrived at work:

I spotted a guy in shorts, T-shirt, and tennis shoes jogging around the warehouse every morning. A big, athletic guy. I asked somebody, "Who's that?"

"That's our CEO," came the answer. And, of course, later in the day, I'd see the same guy, walking around the warehouse, talking with everybody, getting ideas for the business, only by then he'd changed into a suit.

"Everybody wanted to be around Harry," Suzanne Busey Cosper recalls. She was hired in Ingram's credit department staff in 1973 and became one of five female vice presidents before she left twenty years later. "Harry was drop-dead handsome, and his wife Norma was beautiful. He looked like a movie star. But I never saw that guy talk down to a single person. He treated everybody with respect."

Wyatt "Buddy" Pickler joined the organization in 1978 as the systems project leader, which means that his time at Ingram overlapped only briefly with Hoffman's. Yet he says Hoffman left an indelible impression on him. Pickler remembers Hoffman as an impressive yet affable figure at the La Vergne headquarters. "Harry," Pickler recalled, "was a big teddy bear who dominated the room."

In the minds of many people, Ingram Book Company and Harry Hoffman were almost synonymous. But in December of 1978, Harry made the decision to move on.

* * *

It was already a year of great stress for the Ingram family. In 1977, Bronson and his older brother Fritz Ingram had been indicted in Chicago on corruption charges unrelated to the book company. The case concerned an Ingram Barge Company contract with Chicago's Metropolitan Sanitary District. Bronson was acquitted, but Fritz was convicted of bribery for payments made to Chicago government officials. He served sixteen months in a minimum security federal prison at Eglin Air Force Base before having his sentence commuted by President Jimmy Carter. The whole experience of this very public episode, of course, was traumatic for the Ingram family, which had long valued its privacy.

The Chicago trial and the conviction of Fritz led to an Ingram family decision to restructure its business holdings, with Bronson forming in 1978 a new entity called Ingram Industries Inc. This became the parent company over the book and barge businesses, headquartered in Nashville, with Bronson as its chairman. The oil and refining businesses, led by Fritz, would be based in New Orleans.

Given all that was happening in the larger family enterprise, 1978 was not a convenient time to lose the book company's president. But in early December, Hoffman was offered the CEO job at Walden Book Company, owner of

Waldenbooks, which was at that time the leading owner of mall-based bookstores across the United States. Pfeffer remembers Hoffman coming to him for help.

"Harry and I had gotten to be very good friends," Pfeffer remembers. "And then one Tuesday afternoon he says to me that he's been offered the job of president and CEO of Waldenbooks, and that he's accepted it. He wanted my help writing a letter of resignation that he would send to Bronson."

Perhaps Hoffman wanted to announce his resignation in written form because he was a bit intimidated by Bronson's somewhat formidable personality. Bronson was a big presence, not someone to be taken lightly by colleagues and subordinates. Pfeffer himself, while describing Bronson as his "best friend" and saying, "I've never been as close to anyone as I was to him," also recalls that, when he joined the company, he was the very first person to call Bronson by his first name: "Everyone else called him Mr. Ingram."

Still, Pfeffer sensed that an impersonal letter would not be the right way for Hoffman to handle the situation, especially given the recent trauma the family business had experienced. "Harry," he said, "you've worked with Bronson for how many years?"

"About ten years," Hoffman replied.

"You need to go see Bronson," Pfeffer said. "You need to tell him you're resigning, and why you're resigning, and what you're gonna be doing. Harry, you've worked with Bronson for a long time. You've had a wonderful relationship. You need to go and see him in person."

So Hoffman requested a private meeting with Bronson, which he recalls as brief and disappointing.

He described the CEO position that Waldenbooks was offering him. He remembers telling Ingram he would prefer to continue as before, but would appreciate a bump in his salary. "I went to Bronson. I was making $100,000 a year. I said I'd been offered $375,000. I said, 'Can you help me out a little bit? I really don't want to go.' And Bronson turned me down. He said 'The highest paid guy I have is making $100,000. I can't give you more than him.'"

So Hoffman accepted the new job and left Ingram Book Company before the end of the year. He took up his new duties as CEO of Waldenbooks in January 1979. The man who had become the face of Ingram Book Company was now moving from La Vergne, Tennessee, to a new corner office in Stamford, Connecticut.

Pfeffer expected there would be a national search to find Hoffman's replacement. That was not to be. Within minutes of the end of his meeting with Hoffman, Bronson phoned Pfeffer.

The chairman, in his matter-of-fact way, said, "Okay, Harry resigned, I didn't expect it. I've got all these things going on. I'd like you to help on an interim basis. Come to my office tomorrow at noon, and we'll have lunch." Pfeffer told me that last detail was unusual; it was the first time Pfeffer had ever been invited to lunch by Bronson.

In preparation for their lunchtime discussion, Pfeffer sketched out a one-page list of interim organizational considerations separate from launching an executive search process. He recalls what happened next:

> I came to Bronson's office the next day, and we got in a car and drive over to his house, which was a stone's throw from the Ingram office. Back then, we didn't have a corporate dining room. Bronson usually ate his meals alone at home. I remember, he sat at one end of the dining room table and I sat at the other. Before lunch was served, he said he wanted to ask me two questions.
>
> "First, do you think you can run Ingram Book Company?"
>
> "I think I can," I replied.
>
> "Second question. Do you want to run Ingram Book Company?"
>
> "Yes," I said.
>
> "Very well," Bronson said. "You're the president and CEO of Ingram Book Company. Let's eat lunch. I'll meet you out at the book company at three this afternoon, and we'll tell everybody else."

Phil Pfeffer was thirty-four years old. In various roles, he would help lead Ingram Book Company and its expanding ventures for the next twenty years.

* * *

As for Hoffman, he went on to serve as CEO of Waldenbooks for twelve years, during which time the chain grew from five hundred stores to thirteen hundred and quadrupled its sales. Innovative as ever, he created a Preferred Reader program that, within a year, attracted 3.8 million members who accounted for 35 percent of the chain's total sales. He also expanded the chain's distribution capabilities by opening a second warehouse—in La Vergne, Tennessee, literally next door to Ingram's flagship facility. What could be a more convenient location for Walden to enjoy rapid, inexpensive replenishment from the stock of the world's biggest and best book wholesaler?

When Hoffman announced his retirement from Waldenbooks in 1991, the *New York Times* quoted praise from publishing leaders like Laurence Kirshbaum, president of Warner Books, who called Hoffman "one of the giants of the business," and Peter Mayer, chairman of the Penguin Group, later observed that Hoffman had "changed the book industry."

Those encomiums surely pleased Hoffman. But looking back on his career decades later, he chose to quote a different compliment from the same year. "Bronson Ingram invited me to join him at the 1991 Super Bowl in Tampa," Hoffman recalled. "He was hosting a meeting that included all the leaders of the businesses that Ingram had acquired over the years. And I remember he told those executives, 'If it wasn't for Harry Hoffman, none of you guys would be here.' To have Bronson Ingram say that about me was one of the crowning moments of my career."

In 1998, Hoffman published a little book of leadership tips. Titled *The Pocket Mentor: Essential Advice for Aspiring Executives*, it runs just 154 pages but contains a rich trove of stories and useful recommendations for young businesspeople who hope to rise in the corporate ranks.

The book's brevity reflects Hoffman's own philosophy about books. Those who worked with him recall that Hoffman liked to complain about the excessive size of so many of the books publishers delivered to him and his customers. He wasn't wrong: Most publishers will admit that too many books, especially in the nonfiction arena, are little more than magazine articles puffed up to three hundred pages just to justify a bigger package and a higher price. When Hoffman got the chance to write his own book, he practiced what he'd preached.

Pfeffer wrote the foreword for Hoffman's book. In it, he captured some of the qualities that made Hoffman such a powerful force in the growth of Ingram:

> Harry didn't get into a lot of detail, but he had an amazing ability to skim through a great deal of information, get to the top of it, and then focus on key issues. At our daily meeting, he always offered or tuned up what we began to call the "idea of the day." He would say, "Here's an idea, how can we approach it, does it make any sense?" The tremendous success of Ingram was in large part due to those ideas. Maybe only 10 percent of them were ever implemented, but because of the creative environment, there were so many ideas we could pursue.

And after summarizing some of the innovations that Hoffman brought to the book business, beginning with the microfiche-based catalog, Pfeffer concluded, "In my opinion, Harry has done more to get 'books to readers' than probably anyone else in the twentieth century with the possible exception of Oprah Winfrey."

The ability to be a *smart* risk-taker, and the judgment required to distinguish powerful innovations from possible disasters, was one of the gifts that made Hoffman a special business leader. But not every new idea that Hoffman implemented at Ingram was successful. In *The Pocket Mentor*, Hoffman describes one of his failures: a deal he made during his first year at the helm of Ingram with a company called Vinabind. Vinabind's specialty was removing the front and back covers of paperback books and replacing them with laminated cardboard covers, transforming the paperbacks into sturdy books that were the equivalent of hardcovers. Hoffman believed the Vinabind process could enable Ingram to greatly increase its library sales, since libraries were reluctant to buy paperback books they perceived as fragile. He arranged for Vinabind to convert thousands of paperbacks into hardcovers—only to discover that Ingram's library customers were uninterested in buying them. Hoffman was crestfallen. "Thousands of dollars that we could ill afford were wasted, as well as a great deal of time and effort."

One of the qualities that made Hoffman an unusually successful businessperson is that he understood how to convert this sort of failure into a valuable learning experience. "In order to bring innovation and ideas to your company," he concluded, "you must be a risk-taker, but you must also make sure that you have exposed your idea or plan to intensive thought and research. Instincts play an important role when deciding to implement an idea, but if you have not also developed a well-thought-out plan, the tolerance for your failures will diminish."

The Vinabind failure taught Hoffman how to do a better job of judging the potential of innovative ideas—a talent he applied effectively in his future career, both at Ingram and at Waldenbooks. For example, in his own book's account of the success of microfiche, Hoffman declares, "I did not employ a brilliant strategy to achieve this goal. Instead, I 'put myself in the customer's shoes'—in this case, the shoes of the retail bookseller. Being aware of the retailer's needs was my top priority." Thus, Hoffman's gregarious personality, his ability to listen attentively to others, and his readiness to adopt the perspective of other people were keys to his skill at innovation—more so than any creative genius he may have had.

Even more important, the experience of failure helped Hoffman develop empathy and tolerance for imperfection among those working with him. "I found people to be understanding of my mistake," he wrote. "I believe they felt encouraged to take chances themselves because they knew that if they were to fail in some endeavor, they would not be chastised or penalized."

Hoffman was above all a people person. If his talent as a manager in the publishing industry could be ascribed to any one quality, it would be his interest in the people he worked with, his empathy for them, and his ability to understand their needs and interests. Hoffman himself used the word "love" to describe this attitude: "[W]hen I had the good fortune to secure a job in the book business," he wrote, "I found that I really loved this business. My association with book publishers, book retailers, and book wholesalers was always enjoyable. My love for the business helped immeasurably in advancing my career."

Harry Hoffman's ability to infuse this instinctive sense of caring—of love— into his colleagues at Ingram was a crucial part of his legacy. He died in June 2020, at the age of ninety-two, having left an indelible mark on the Ingram business and the entire publishing industry.

7

THE INGRAM FAMILY'S IMPACT

Soon after Harry Hoffman's departure, the new boss of the book company, Phil Pfeffer, set an ambitious revenue goal to end the decade. The slogan he coined was "Ninety-nine in seventy-nine"—in other words, to reach $99 million in revenues by the end of 1979. Ingram Book Company achieved the goal—in fact, the sales total for 1979 was $105 million, almost triple the $36 million achieved just two years earlier, in 1977.

A profile in the *Nashville Banner* (October 18, 1979), put the Ingram Book Company story in the context of Bronson Ingram's career as leader of the broader family business:

> DiMaggio in center field, Landowska on the cello—talent always makes it look easy. With E. Bronson Ingram, it's a deep and silent talent for making money…
>
> In his mid-40s, Bronson speaks like someone who was schooled to speak his mind—and who understands the assets of silence. He is built like a middleweight and wears a permanent tan earned on boat decks and fairways…
>
> Bronson's barges ply the veins and arteries of America's heartland. About 500 barges, tugs and towboats carry a variety of natural products from Pittsburgh west to Omaha or Tulsa; from St. Paul south to New Orleans and onto the Mexican border through the intercoastal waterways.
>
> They carry coal and oil, sand and gravel—much of it produced by Ingram mines, wells and pits…
>
> Bronson's Ingram Industries includes Ingram Barge Co., Acadian Sand & Limestone, Ingram Materials (sand), Ingram Coal Co., Ingram Book Co., Bluewater Insurance Ltd., an insurance company, and Gulfco Industries, maker of oil well valves.
>
> All are operated under an umbrella of ownership by the Ingrams—with only about 10 percent in the hands of a few of Ingram's 1,500 employees.
>
> It all seems to be working. Early this year *Fortune* magazine placed

the Ingram brothers among 62 Americans they termed "the elusive, private rich." Their net worth was estimated at about $100 million.

The *Banner* reporter noted that Bronson seemed most absorbed in two of the family businesses in particular—the coal company, which Bronson viewed as a potentially important part of America's ongoing quest for affordable energy sources, and the rapidly growing book business. The journalist went on to briefly summarize the remarkable story of Ingram Book Company—launched as a favor to a friend, then built into the country's largest book wholesaler, already enjoying annual sales of $100 million.

The *Banner* story focused mainly on Bronson—understandably, since he had become, while still a young man of forty-eight, one of Tennessee's most successful business leaders. He'd developed and begun practicing a remarkable range of management and leadership skills: decisiveness, clarity of focus, understanding of risk and how to control it, and unshakable integrity.

Those who worked with Bronson still talk about the qualities that made him an effective CEO. Steve Little, who served Ingram for sixteen years in a range of executive roles, says he developed the habit of presenting new ideas to Bronson in the form of brief, written memos. "This way, Bronson could reflect on the idea as a whole before discussing it with you," Little says. "And there was never a single time when he didn't add value in the process. He would always say, 'Have you thought about this? What about considering that?' And the points he raised were always worthwhile and important."

Bronson's wife Martha was mentioned in the *Banner* story mainly in terms of her civic involvement, including her successful fundraising campaign for the Tennessee Performing Arts Center in Nashville. Unmentioned was Martha's burgeoning role within Ingram Industries—though this is an aspect of her life, and of the Ingram story, that many people associated with the business are happy to talk about.

Martha's direct involvement with the business took off in 1979, shortly after her effort to help launch the new Tennessee Performing Arts Center had come to a successful conclusion. When Bronson asked his wife, "What are you going to do now?" she admitted that she had no real plans.

"Well, would you consider coming to work for me?" Bronson responded.

Martha was hesitant at first about going to work with her husband. *Twenty-four hours a day together. This may not be good for us,* she thought. But she agreed to give it a try. Bronson set aside an office for Martha. "I didn't even have a job description," she recalls, "but I came one day and I never left. I kept finding things to do to help him."

The role that Martha created for herself grew directly out of her personality, which was energetic, observant, gregarious, and empathetic. Although the term was little used in American business at the time, Martha became, in effect, the Ingram Industries ombudsman—a spokesperson for the interests and needs of the people who made up the Ingram community.

In her 2001 book about Bronson, Martha explains how it came about:

> People would talk to me about things that they would never talk to [Bronson] about, such as employee benefits. I sat in on meetings, and someone might ask, "Is my wife covered if we have a baby?" That's very definitely covered by the company's policy, explained in our manuals, but some people weren't aware of it. One long-term associate in the barge company explained to me that those who work with their hands don't read much. It became quite apparent that we needed to have more Quality Circle-type activities and a stronger Human Resources Department.
>
> Then when we first went to the open office concept with no solid walls, people complained to me about the secondhand smoke. I brought it up to him, and Bronson protested, "We've got to let people smoke. This is a free country." (This was before there was an antismoking movement.) I insisted, "Bronson, you're in an enclosed office, and you don't have to deal with the smoke, but these other people do. Now come with me, and let me show you the haze over these offices." When he realized how bad it was, he said, "Oh, my God, this is terrible." So we put in a smoking ban, other than in heavily ventilated break rooms. Even those are now extinct. That is just an example of something I could do for our associates that they would not bring up to him.

Gradually, Martha's role in the company grew and became formalized. She was moved into an office next door to Bronson's own, and she was invited to attend more and more of the major organizational meetings led by her husband. Realizing that a title would add heft to her voice within the business, Martha asked for and received the designation of director of public affairs.

Eventually, in 1984, Martha's job was transformed from a volunteer position to a paid one. The change was triggered indirectly by Tennessee governor Lamar Alexander. A moderate Republican whom Bronson himself had enthusiastically supported, Alexander sent an emissary to ask Martha whether she would consider taking a full-time job in state government as the chancellor of the board of regents of Tennessee's university and community colleges—in effect, the CEO of the entire system.

Alexander and the Tennessee legislature had recently been through a major revision of education policy and had approved full funding of the state's higher education systems. Alexander remembers he was therefore "trying to think outside the box" about a suitable chief executive. (He had previously offered the job to Navy Admiral William Anderson, a Nashville native who was then commandant of the US Naval Academy.) Though flattered by the offer and its six-figure salary, Martha declined the position.

> I started remembering that Bronson was counting on me for more and more things to help him in the ombudsman role for the entire company. But I could not wait to tell Bronson of this amazing meeting, and he noticed that I seemed to have liked the idea of a salary. It was a good feeling to know that I had commercial value.
>
> Bronson picked up his desk phone, called the payroll department and said, "Put Martha R. Ingram on the payroll." Then, turning to me, he asked, "What were they going to pay you?" I told him, and he then mentioned that same number to the payroll person.
>
> That was the beginning of my paid career at Ingram Industries— a memorable moment, for me at least.

Martha did find it ironic when Ingram presented her with a five-year service pin on the fifth anniversary of her first paycheck. "That was odd to me," she says in her book, "because the previous unpaid years at Ingram Industries didn't seem to count because I hadn't received a salary."

In 1981, Martha joined the board of directors of Ingram Industries, further solidifying her important role in shaping the future of the business. She went on to expand her ombudsman role to include acting as an internal representative for Ingram's customers—a kind of customer service manager who has unusual clout, because she bears the same name as the company itself. In her book, Martha describes the pleasure she took in playing this problem-solving role:

> Whenever I am out of town, I'll find a bookstore and go in and ask employees or managers, without identifying myself, "Do you get any books from Ingram?" They invariably say yes, either a lot or most. Then I'll ask if the company does a good job. Sometimes they'll say something like, "I wish they would arrange the invoice alphabetically instead of numerically." Occasionally, I have been able to take those messages back and have them accommodated. At a bookstore in Nantucket where I was recently, they remembered when I was there a

couple of years ago. The manager said, "I couldn't believe it. Within a week of your being here last time the invoices were reversed to the way we wanted them."

Martha sums it up this way: "I have always felt very involved in the business, especially the bookstore part, because I love to read and I love bookstores and libraries." Evidently booksellers and consumers have benefited from Martha's personal commitment to improving the way books get from publishers and into the hands of readers—a key element in the Ingram Book Company's long-term success. Equally important, Martha's commitment to listening to customers, understanding their needs, and taking steps to ensure those needs were met reinforced a vital element in Ingram's corporate culture. When "the boss's wife" demonstrates through personal behavior that caring about customers really matters, you can bet that people throughout the company learn to act the same way.

* * *

BRONSON, HIS BROTHER FRITZ, AND Martha had represented the third generation of Ingrams to be active in the family business. They wouldn't be the last. In the 1970s, during their teen years, the four offspring of Bronson and Martha—sons Orrin, John, and David, and daughter Robin—would all play varying roles in Ingram Industries.

Over many years, Bronson insisted that his three sons in particular have actual working experience in one or more of the family's businesses during their summertime school breaks. Orrin, John, and David each clearly remember their father's instruction about this: "Half your summer belongs to you," he told them, "and the other half belongs to me."

"He gave us a mandate," Orrin recalls. "We had to work at least a month every summer somewhere—and he wanted us to work in our family-owned businesses, if we so chose. He thought it would be a good way to let us learn what working was like, but also to learn a little bit about what put food on the table for the family. John and I were both big into showing horses back then. Dad said he'd be happy to support that, but that a month every summer we were to be working."

The summer work for Orrin began in 1974, when he was fourteen years old. He would report at eight a.m. to Ingram Materials Company, on the east bank of the Cumberland River opposite downtown Nashville. This company was a major supplier of construction sand and gravel to builders across middle Tennessee. Orrin's first assignment was weeding the sand piles.

His next posting, the following summer, was with the book company. He joined in with the regular associates, picking books in the company warehouse in Nashville for shipment to bookstores, libraries, and schools. Orrin was more interested in working aboard the Ingram Barge Company's towboats, but at the time no one under eighteen was permitted to work on the boats. He finally got aboard in 1978 when he was a student at Vanderbilt University.

Orrin remembers how, early on, the captain of the boat figured he ought to keep the boss's son close by and safe.

"Initially, out on the boats, they weren't letting me work, and I complained about it. It only took me a day to tell the captain, 'Look, I'm not going to spend thirty days riding in the pilot house.' So I became a deck-hand, and I cleaned the stove in the galley every night. I made the captain's bed and the chief engineer's bed. I did all those tasks."

In June 2014, Orrin would become the chairman and CEO of Ingram Barge.

John and David Ingram worked multiple summers in the cavernous book warehouses, which was a different sort of manual labor, where the main tasks were preparing shipments to fill customer orders: picking books off their assigned shelves, packing them into cardboard boxes, and placing the boxes on conveyers that led to waiting trucks destined for unseen bookstores.

The work was tedious and often exhausting. But the Ingram brothers never used their family name as an excuse to work any less hard than their colleagues. "They took the job seriously," says Johnny Secrest, who worked alongside each of them back then. "They sweated in the hot warehouse like the rest of us, working like crazy."

David did find ways to bring a touch of creativity to the job. He remembers coming up with a new tool that actually solved a technical problem in the warehouse and made the packing process more efficient. Published books come in many different dimensions, and essentially every customer order has a unique assortment and quantity count. At the time, the boxes used in the Ingram warehouse came in two sizes. This meant it was tricky, like piecing a puzzle together, to assemble a selection of books so that it would fit into the right-sized box.

David's invention was to fashion a modified T-square, cut from heavy cardboard, that sped up the assembling of different-sized book orders. Secrest recalls that the measuring device David developed was actually in use for many years. "They were adopted by everyone at all of our facilities," Secrest says. "They were eventually made out of wood, then plastic. Today we use cubic dimensions, not inches, but at the time they sure were handy."

So all three of Bronson's sons paid their dues in the book company warehouses, packing hardcover and paperback books into cartons that would be shipped to bookstores around the country, only to be opened and sorted by clerks or managers who probably never suspected that a member of the Ingram family had personally handled the contents.

As for their younger sister Robin Ingram, most of her stint in the family business would be spent in the video company—and that introduces a story of product diversification and market expansion that requires its own chapter.

* * *

In these ways, Bronson laid a foundation for this family business—how the enterprise should be managed and how family members, especially those from the next generation, should be engaged in it. A further aspect was his insistence that the business remain private, not only in its ownership basis and structure, but also in avoiding unnecessary publicity.

Bronson explained this philosophy in an interview with *Advantage*, the Nashville business magazine, in April 1987, when he became the board president of the Nashville Area Chamber of Commerce:

> I'm a relatively private person and I've never gotten any particular kicks from blowing my horn and reading about myself on a regular basis as some people do. Some of them overdo it. They usually have some motive for it and think it's going to get them somewhere. It's never gotten me anywhere I wanted to go. I guess I've just never had any interest in it.
>
> My father always believed in being a very quiet person in terms of his accomplishments. He was very active in a lot of things and did a tremendous amount of business. So did my mother. But they did it anonymously. They got their pleasure out of doing it and not out of rubbing anybody's nose in it or taking credit for it. I've been very fortunate. I was born lucky and I've been lucky ever since. I worked very hard at it but I feel like I owe a lot of it back. I try to give financially and with my time. But I don't want any credit for it. It's something I owe. As far as business is concerned, I know what we do and our people know what we do...I don't need to read about what the hell we do and how we do it in a newspaper or a magazine.

To this day, Ingram Industries follows the same approach to publicity as Bronson—which helps explain how Ingram has managed to become one of the most influential companies in book publishing while remaining all but unknown among the vast majority of book readers.

8
What Ships Like a Book?

As Ingram Book Company moved into its second decade, the business was now on solid financial footing. Book publishers and retail booksellers had learned they could count on this wholesaler in Tennessee.

The company was becoming well known inside the US book trade as an essential wholesale connection. As a result of Ingram innovations, beginning with the microfiche inventory management system, the entire trade book business was becoming more efficient. Booksellers and readers alike were discovering that they could get quick, easy, reliable access to the books they wanted anywhere in the country rather than having to wait weeks for shipments from distant publisher warehouses. Ingram was the key link in the chain that made this possible.

Ingram Book Company was also becoming a notable employer in middle Tennessee. Hiring at Ingram reflected this new level of acceptance in the industry. In 1970, there had been only eighteen employees at the book company. By 1987, the total employment would be more than eighteen hundred associates.

By this time, that all-hands-on-deck internal attitude now permeated Ingram Book Company. And the spirit of "Do whatever it takes" was not only reflected in holiday-season warehouse assignments. It was expressed in many other ways.

Kent Freeman, who joined the company in 1982 as a young software engineer, offers one example. Freeman was part of an information systems team led by Buddy Pickler. Another member of that team was Charles Levy, who managed the so-called mainframe environment on the giant IBM computer, which then housed all of Ingram's business data.

Early in Freeman's tenure, Levy announced that he'd been offered a great job at IBM, and that he'd soon be departing Ingram. This created an opening for Freeman—except he acknowledged that he didn't have the background knowledge or experience needed to fill Levy's shoes. No problem: At Pickler's suggestion, Levy and Freeman both volunteered to come into the Ingram offices every Saturday for about a year, so that Levy could train Freeman in how to manage the big IBM mainframe.

Freeman's enthusiasm for the technological challenges he faced at Ingram led to other notable feats of dedication. He quickly became one of the leaders of Ingram's effort to develop software and communications tools that would let booksellers send their product orders to Ingram electronically. Today, on more advanced computing systems, this is a relatively simple task. But that wasn't true with the much more primitive systems available in the early 1980s. The Ingram information technology team had to write and rewrite code to make the appropriate file transfers possible—and at first, it took many hours for the orders to be transmitted, recorded at Ingram, and then confirmed by a return computer message sent back to the bookstore.

A big leap forward became possible in 1983, when IBM began marketing something called the 3270 emulator—a circuit board that could duplicate the functions of an IBM 3270 mainframe computer terminal on a PC or other microcomputer. Freeman describes what happened next:

> I got the manual, and I read it, and I got so excited that I pulled an all-nighter, I wrote a proof-of-concept code—in other words, a software program that would let the little computer in a bookstore talk directly with Ingram's mainframe. The next morning, I came in and showed Buddy how it could work. The trend was unmistakable. "Dude," I said to Buddy, "the curve says we're heading from next day to eight hours to four hours and soon we're going be at same-call confirmation." In other words, a bookseller would soon be able to place an order and get immediate confirmation from Ingram. And that was a big, big deal. It became the basis of what we called Flashback—our electronic ordering service that included same-call confirmation.

Freeman notes that "pulling an all-nighter wasn't unusual for me." Freeman's readiness to make such extraordinary efforts undoubtedly reflects his youthful energy as well as the excitement he felt over being a player in a technological revolution. But it also reflected the family business ethic that characterized all of Ingram Industries, and in particular the Ingram Book Company.

In 1980, Bronson Ingram elevated Phil Pfeffer to executive vice president of the parent company, Ingram Industries Inc., and also put him on the corporate board of directors. They named David Williams, then an officer at Ingram Barge Company, the new president of the Ingram Book Company. Williams would serve in that role until 1983.

Pfeffer, however, continued to play an important role in shaping the strategy of the book company. The Pfeffer years at Ingram—the 1980s and 1990s, more or less—would be a kind of "golden age" for the book business, one that built on the legacy of Harry Hoffman with fresh innovations, expansion into new markets, ever-deepening relationships with customers, and impressive growth. Pfeffer surely deserves his share of the credit for these developments. And while Pfeffer has said that Bronson seemed to regard the success of the Ingram Book Company as largely a matter of good luck (Pfeffer is quoted to that effect in Martha Ingram's book about her husband), smart, strategic thinking was at least as important. That kind of thinking wouldn't have happened without the effective partnership of Bronson and Pfeffer.

* * *

In 1981, Bronson and Pfeffer began exploring the potential for a new kind of growth based on a very practical question: what new products *other than books* might bookstores offer their customers, and that Ingram might also provide and thus maximize the value of its own functioning supply chain?

Internally, this search for what a marketing strategist might call "complementary product categories" would be framed in several ways. One was "What ships like a book?" In other words, what other products might also fit into the boxes that Ingram was regularly shipping to booksellers around the country? What products could fit alongside books on the Ingram warehouse shelves, keep the company's shipping cartons full, and enable booksellers to diversify their own product offerings, thereby fueling their business growth and profitability? As Pfeffer put it to *Forbes* writer Randall Lane for an Ingram Industries company profile in 1994, "A box is a box." Why not fill that box with as many profitable items as possible?

"We were running fast, we were making money," Pfeffer explained in an interview years later. "We'd made the book business profitable. The cash flow was good. And then Bronson wanted us to do other things, kind of working off of the distribution business. We had learned a lot about putting things in boxes, getting the orders right, getting the products to customers quickly, and on and on. We knew we were very good at all these tasks. And so we began to talk about other things that look like books, feel like books, and ship like books."

Two product categories in particular attracted the attention of the Ingram team—videocassettes of feature films and software for personal computers, which were then emerging as an important tool for small businesses, families, and students. Each of these product categories had its own complexities, including special distribution systems, a fragmented national network of distributors and retailers, and distinct marketing and promotional challenges.

"In my conversations with Bronson," Pfeffer remembers, "one of the first things we talked about was prerecorded videocassettes. The reason was that a prerecorded videocassette, whether it was in the Beta or VHS format, actually looked like a book. It could ship like a book. It could be inventoried like a book. That meant all of the logistical systems that we had developed to help us serve booksellers could work for prerecorded videocassettes."

But could Ingram carve out a sizable, profitable niche in this new and different line of business? There were a number of challenges that would need to be addressed.

One problem was that not many theatrical films were being released by the studios for sale to the general public. At the time, Pfeffer remembers, most of the available products were X-rated films. "And as we embarked on this, I remember very clearly Martha Ingram saying, 'No R-rated, no X-rated products.' Fortunately, in time she relented on the R-rated films, because, as it turned out, so many popular movies were rated R."

In addition, in those early days of the video business, the cost of videotapes was quite high, averaging a hundred dollars or more. This discouraged booksellers, especially the smaller independent stores, from stocking them. Thus, most of the market for movie videotapes was restricted to storefront shops that rented the tapes for a few dollars per night—with pornography generating a significant slice of the industry's revenues.

Another problem was that the sales and distribution system for videotapes was fragmented and inefficient. Because the major movie studios—Columbia, Warner Brothers, Universal, and so on—all had their own record companies, they had entered into deals with local music distributors to sell videotapes as well. So the company that delivered records to record shops in Dallas was also the video distributor for Dallas, while other companies had the same roles in San Antonio, Nashville, Denver, Miami, and elsewhere.

The lack of a national wholesaler or distributor made it very difficult to develop and execute a national sales and marketing strategy for video—much as the book business had been severely hampered by the lack of a national distribution system prior to the rise of Ingram. To overcome this problem, Ingram would have to convince the movie studios to abandon the local distributors and hand this business over to them—a tricky proposition, since movie executives had no experience in the book business and therefore no knowledge of Ingram.

Thus, the mere fact that a videotape could ship like a book didn't automatically translate into a product line that made sense for Ingram.

Similarly, the computer software business was attractive, since PCs were emerging as an important tool for small businesses, families, and students, but that market presented some challenges of its own.

One challenge was the fact that retailers who were selling the early software packages—including primitive but then-groundbreaking productivity tools such as VisiCalc, Lotus 1-2-3, and WordPerfect—represented yet another set of businesses, separate from both the booksellers whom Ingram knew well and the video retailers who would be the prime market for videotapes. These computer-oriented retailers were interested in selling computer hardware, related equipment like printers and monitors, and accessories as well as software. A wholesaler that handled just one segment of their product array wouldn't be a very attractive business partner, since it wouldn't add much efficiency to their supply chain management.

So these two businesses handling ships-like-a-book products posed thorny business challenges for Ingram. Figuring out whether expanding into the video and software industries would make strategic and financial sense required diligent planning and fact-based research. To lead this strategic exploration, Phil Pfeffer identified Mike Fine.

Fine had already spent a lifetime immersed in the worlds of books and publishing. As a college student in New York, he courted his future wife, Marlene, as the two of them browsed the aisles of the Eighth Street Bookshop in Greenwich Village. In 1960, they were both accepted to the famous University of Iowa Writers' Workshop (Marlene as a poet, Mike as a playwright) and attended together for six months—until Mike quit the program in order to open up one of the country's first paperback-only bookstores, across the street from the university. Later, Fine became part-owner of the Paperback Forum, a famous New York bookstore across the street from Columbia University, where the customers included the likes of James Baldwin, Lionel Trilling, and Susan Sontag.

In the 1970s, Fine created Bookthrift, a wholesaler of remainder books and a bargain book publisher that was later acquired by Simon & Schuster. Both remainders and bargain books involve titles published by mainstream publishers that, for one reason or another, stop selling at full retail price. Remainder houses like Bookthrift buy the unsold inventory from publishers at bargain-basement prices, then sell it to bookstores to be retailed at discount. Companies like Bookthrift would also sometimes arrange to reprint books, again for sale on the bargain-book tables of bookstores.

Every major book retailer had become a customer of Bookthrift, and Fine was seen as a canny entrepreneur who could identify growth opportunities in and around the book business. So it was natural for Ingram to reach out to Fine in 1981 seeking advice on the potential for the video and software businesses.

"After Ingram called me," Fine remembers, "I planned a trip to Nashville where I had a meeting with Bronson Ingram—the first time I had met him. I knew something of Ingram, of course. I certainly knew Harry Hoffman and Mike Zibart. And I knew the company's amazing success story—how, in ten years, it had grown from a tiny business into a $125-million book wholesaler."

In their meeting, Bronson was highly focused on the strategic help he needed. Fine recalls, "He started the conversation by saying, 'You're here because you're a candidate to help lead a new strategic arm of the company, which I want to call Ingram Ventures.'"

"And then he leaned in and said to me, 'Mike, you've been recommended to me as one of the best entrepreneurs in the book business. But I want you to know that we don't have to be in the book business. We can do anything. We can be in airlines. We can be in railroads. We can be in oil. We can be in drilling. We can be in steel.' It was a long list of major industries."

Bronson wanted to make it clear that Fine would have carte blanche to recommend almost any kind of market or product expansion that made business sense for Ingram. And Fine was impressed by Bronson's personality. "Bronson was pragmatic," Fine says. "He was witty. He was practical to the extreme. He was attentive. He was tough. He was extremely acute and rational. In fact, from everything that I could see, Bronson Ingram was simply a very, very good businessman."

Fine left the meeting with an invitation from Bronson to propose new lines of business for Ingram. "He didn't know what I would come back with," Fine says. "I came back with enthusiasm for the explosion of the about-to-happen video business and the about-to-happen personal computer business. And I made the case for Bronson's taking his expertise in book distribution and applying it to those product categories."

Fine and Bronson agreed that Fine would leave Simon & Schuster to become president of the new Ingram Ventures. Recruiting Fine illustrated a strategy that Ingram would practice with increasing frequency and success in the years to come—strategic hiring specifically focused on bringing in the specialized talent needed to fuel innovation, diversification, and growth.

Fine proceeded to flesh out his diversification plan for Ingram Book Company. Fine's plan emphasized the fact that both the video and the PC software businesses were still in their infancy.

"You have to realize that Steve Jobs had started Apple in 1975, just six years earlier," Fine recalls.

And it was only in 1981 that IBM created the first PC and started its conversations with Bill Gates about creating what would become the Windows platform. At the same time, the technology for viewing films on videotape was just arriving in American homes. There were a hundred million TV households in America—and, by 1981, three million of them had VCRs. They were about to explode into every household in America. And yet there was almost zero product to serve this new market, and very few video stores equipped to bring video products to customers. This was a huge opportunity, though it had yet to be clearly defined.

As part of his research to define this opportunity more clearly, Fine visited marketing officials for many companies in the movie industry—big names like MGM, Columbia, Paramount, Warner, 20th Century Fox, and Walt Disney—none of whom had ever heard of Ingram. He found that these entertainment companies had not figured out how they wanted to market copies of their valuable movie content. What would be the most profitable balance between videotape rentals and sales? What kinds of retail outlets would market the videotapes, and on what terms? Who would handle distribution of the products? These were all questions with which movie studios had no prior experience. "They had a tiger by the tail," Fine says.

Similarly, it was unclear exactly how, in the long run, software for PCs would be marketed to consumers. Would software be sold direct to consumers by computer companies? Would it be marketed through electronics stores, appliance stores, office supply stores, or dedicated software retailers? Or would software—which, after all, was a form of intellectual content that was, at the time, packaged in physical containers very similar to books in size, shape, weight, and sometimes even in price—end up becoming a staple on bookstore shelves?

The latter is certainly what Pfeffer believed. In her book, Martha Ingram quotes Pfeffer as saying, "Initially, we got into the software business because we thought the bookstores would be centers for education, entertainment, and information, which would include microcomputer software." And at the time, there was no sound reason for assuming this was wrong. After all, as Pfeffer also remarked, "We didn't know where the microcomputer business was going. Neither did the microcomputer business itself know where it was going."

Under the circumstances, it made sense for forward-thinking businesspeople to look for opportunities to stake claims in a burgeoning business whose exact shape no one could predict. And that's exactly what Ingram did, guided in part by the insights of Fine.

Fine remained with Ingram for three years. His strategic thinking, as communicated to Bronson, became the basis for more than a decade of growth by Ingram in the video and software businesses.

At the time, most outside observers would probably have viewed video and software as a big leap for a company like Ingram, with its roots in oil, raw materials, shipping, and other heavy industries. But looking back on these events from today's perspective, Fine sees some surprising throughlines:

> It's interesting to remember that Bronson's core expertise was the transport of oil and other products on the inland waterways. He was an expert in how to get goods from here to there. The Ingram Book Company was doing something similar with books. Now you change the product base and the customer base, and you see that the video and software businesses are not that far removed from what Bronson had already mastered. And then consider the burgeoning opportunity of how many people would end up wanting and using these products— video programs and computer software. This market would ultimately include virtually every consumer on the planet. So it's no wonder that Bronson Ingram wanted to get involved.
>
> Today, the largest business in the world is the global media business, and the hardest-fought turf battles we're seeing involve the streaming business. And all of this is a direct outgrowth of what Bronson Ingram and I were talking about back in 1981.

One way that Ingram tackled the challenge of a lack of national distribution in the video business was by convincing independent video retailers to make Ingram their main supplier. This was time-consuming work that required plenty of one-on-one conversations with video store owners scattered all over the country. Pfeffer recalls how Ray Capp, who headed the Ingram video sales effort, commemorated his efforts by framing all of the luggage tags from the far-flung cities he'd visited. "By signing up dozens and dozens of video sales partners," Pfeffer says, "we were able to build a national distribution capability for prerecorded videocassettes." Ingram gradually transformed the fragmented, chaotic video market into a unified national marketplace—a process analogous to the one Ingram had driven in the trade book arena.

The new national distribution service also became the main channel for delivery of videocassettes to a new type of store—the video rental shop, or "rentailer." Initially, the movie studios hated and feared the idea of independent businesses renting videocassettes to customers; they sensed these stores would siphon away a significant share of the millions of dollars' worth of value that the studios had invested in creating the movies. The studios even launched legal challenges to the right of the rentailers to exist. But movie rental just made too much economic sense. An entrepreneur could lease a storefront, buy a collection of popular movies at $100 to $135 apiece, then rent them to customers for $5 or $10 a night—a reasonable price to pay to let a family watch the latest movie hit. After twelve or fifteen rentals, the videocassette was paid for, and everything thereafter would be profit for the store owner.

Soon video rental shops began springing up everywhere—and Ingram became the supplier of choice for most of them. In the process, Ingram became the largest distributor of prerecorded videocassettes in the world.

This new growth spurt created new challenges for the Ingram distribution and fulfillment systems. And as with previous challenges, the company responded with creativity and an unusual level of personal commitment from many associates.

Johnny Secrest describes what happened when the video business generated its first giant explosion of demand. It came about not through a movie but a video game. In 1984, Nintendo released its version of *Pac-Man*, one of the first megahits in the genre. A huge flood of packages had to be shipped from the Ingram warehouse to meet the enormous demand. Ray Taylor, then in charge of all of Ingram's distribution services, visited Secrest in the warehouse and asked, "Johnny, are you going to get everything shipped today?"

Secrest answered, "There's no way in hell we're getting all of this out today."

Taylor pressed him: "Well, if that's what you really believe, then maybe we have you in the wrong job."

Secrest was taken aback. "That was eye-opening for me," he recalled years later.

But it was typical Ingram—a moment of candor. And then Taylor put his arm around me and said, "John, do you recognize what you did wrong there?"

"Well, no sir," I said.

"You should have said something like, 'I'm really struggling. I don't know how to do this. I could use some ideas.' If you'd asked for a little help, I'd have told you we can figure out how to get this done."

And the next thing I knew, Ray and I were working out solutions so we could get everything shipped that day.

That was a big learning experience for me. It helped me think differently about my career and about how I could help other folks be successful.

In time, Bronson's youngest son, David, became part of the company's video division. David had worked in the treasury department of Ingram Industries from 1989 to 1991, and had recently earned an MBA degree from the Owen Graduate School of Management at Vanderbilt. Realizing that he needed more experience in one of the company's operating divisions, David decided that he wanted to join the video business, which by then had been given the name Ingram Entertainment Inc.

"My rationale was," he later explained to his mother, "here is a business that would do a little over $300 million, relatively small for a distribution company, at least relatively small compared to the other [Ingram] companies . . . I felt like it was a place that I could make an impact, just because it was a business with probably twelve or fifteen competitors and it was a growing-and-blowing industry."

David worked with Ingram Entertainment's CEO, John Taylor, as well as with Pfeffer to continue the division's growth. In June 1992, the team arranged to purchase Commtron, their biggest competitor at the time. This made Ingram Entertainment the largest video distributor in the country.

By this time, Blockbuster had grown into the dominant video store chain. In September 1993, Blockbuster announced that they were planning to consolidate all of their business with a single distributor. Ingram Entertainment had to decide how to respond. One option would be to go all-in on negotiating a big deal with Blockbuster, which would immediately double Ingram's business with the chain, from around $200 million per year to $400 million.

On the surface, this was an attractive proposition. But just below the surface, it had several problems. One was that Blockbuster was insisting on draconian financial terms—understandably, given the chain's enormous clout in the industry. The new, big deal with Blockbuster would actually generate less profit for Ingram than they'd previously enjoyed. Second, David and the rest of the team sensed—quite accurately—that Blockbuster's move to a single distributor was probably just a way-station on the road to developing the company's own distribution system. Thus, the seemingly rich $400 million revenue stream would likely vanish within a couple of years. Third, on general strategic grounds, the Ingram leaders were hesitant to become overly dependent on a single customer—never a safe or comfortable place to be. In fact, the company management had grown increasingly conscious over time of the importance of diversification to their prospects for financial stability and future growth.

For all these reasons, Ingram Entertainment opted not to compete for the exclusive distributorship with Blockbuster. Ingram lost its $200 million in annual revenues from the chain, but within about a year it made up that sum from expanded deals with other customers. It had been a tricky decision to make, but the instincts of the Ingram leadership team proved to be sound.

Incidentally, Robin Ingram had worked at Ingram's video distribution business for a time during her high school years. But when she graduated from Duke University with a degree in art history, she made a different choice than her brothers. Rather than launching a career with one of the Ingram companies, she asked her father whether he would help her start a business of her own. Bronson agreed, but he was apprehensive when Robin told him her business of choice was an art gallery. "Retailing paintings was not an area of expertise for any of us," Martha observes.

The family arranged to hire an experienced gallery manager named Michael Judge to partner with Robin. The two operated the Ingram-Judge Gallery on the ground floor of Ingram headquarters in Nashville for three years, at which point Robin got married and moved to Boston. In June 1999, she joined the Ingram Industries board.

Fine's plan to move aggressively into video wholesaling helped Ingram launch a big new business. In a similar way, the part of Fine's plan that concerned PC software paved the way for a major growth initiative by Ingram. Fine's recommendations reinforced work that Pfeffer had already been doing with a company based in Buffalo, New York, called Software Distribution Services (SDS). SDS was then the fourth or fifth largest software distributor in the country, with an emphasis on business software. In 1985, an opportunity came for Ingram to buy the privately held SDS. The combined businesses took on the name of Ingram Software.

Then, also in 1985, a California-based public competitor called Micro D, a successful wholesaler of microcomputer products operated by Lynwood "Chip" A. Lacy, became available. Micro D's founders and owners, a husband-and-wife team of schoolteachers named Geza Czige and Lorraine Mecca, had arranged to meet with Pfeffer and Steven J. Mason, who was now the president and CEO of Ingram Book Company.

During a get-to-know-you meeting at the airport, Czige and Mecca told the Ingram team that they were becoming dissatisfied with the business. "The profit margins were coming down from 20 percent to around 10 percent," Mason recalls, "and they just didn't see a future for their business. Phil and I glanced at one another at that point, because we both knew exactly what kind of margins we could make. We sensed that this could be a very attractive deal for Ingram."

After a quick call to get Bronson's approval, Pfeffer acquired for Ingram 51 percent of Micro D for about seven million dollars—roughly two dollars per share. Ingram bought another 10 percent of the company's stock the following year and the remainder in 1989. Renamed Ingram Micro, it would become the largest global distributor of technical products in the world.

That swift acquisition of Micro D illustrates another crucial aspect of Ingram's strategic style: the readiness to move quickly and decisively when a genuinely valuable opportunity emerges. At a glance, this might appear to conflict with the company's generally conservative approach to business finance that emphasizes keeping debt burdens low. In fact, these two traits are complementary. A company that manages its finances prudently—"keeping its powder dry," as the saying goes—has the resources to take advantage of unexpected opportunities without becoming overextended. It's a lesson some of the digital companies of the 1990s—those that expanded too fast and too carelessly, then fell apart in the dot-com bust of 2001—would have done well to learn.

* * *

INGRAM'S EFFORT TO DIVERSIFY ITS product distribution didn't stop with video and software. In the early 1980s, the company launched Ingram Periodicals to deliver weekly and monthly magazines to bookstores. It was another answer to the question—"What ships like a book?"—that had already proven so fruitful.

At the same time that Ingram was expanding its product line, the company was also expanding geographically. "We realized that, in many cases, we could get books from the United States into Australia and New Zealand faster than the American publishers could," Pfeffer said. To serve this new market, Ingram International was created in 1983.

Thus, by the middle of the 1980s, Ingram had begun applying many of the business methods and strategies it originally developed for the American trade book business to other products and markets. To reflect this new, bigger reality, an umbrella business called Ingram Distribution Group was created.

Ingram Book Company thus became a division of the distribution group. In 1983, Mason had replaced Williams as president and CEO of the division. Mason, an attorney, had previously served as general counsel of Ingram Industries. Now he was interested in gaining experience in one of the company's operating divisions.

Mason would spend seven years at the helm of the book company. These would be some of the most eventful years in the history of book publishing.

9

AN INDUSTRY TRANSFORMED

In 1989, as Ingram Book Company turned twenty years old, it reached another remarkable sales milestone. Company revenues in 1970 had been about one million dollars. By 1980, they'd grown to more than $100 million. Now, in 1989, the total surpassed one billion dollars. This included about $400 million in book sales and another $600 million in combined video and software revenues.

Ingram's growth reflected a series of transformations that were affecting the entire book business during the 1980s and early 1990s—transformations that Ingram itself had helped make possible. These changes included the continued rapid growth of book retailing, especially through the expansion of the bookstore chains. Waldenbooks, which had grown to 250 stores by 1977, was purchased by Kmart in 1984, then merged with the smaller Borders chain in 1992, creating a giant network of 1,289 bookstores across the country. B. Dalton, which had expanded into 43 states by 1978, continued to open stores during the 1980s, reaching a peak of 798 stores by 1986. In 1977, businessman Robert Haft founded the Crown Books discount chain with a single store in Washington, DC. By 1991, Crown had grown to 257 stores, making it then the third largest bookstore chain in the United States (trailing only Barnes & Noble and Waldenbooks).

As the 1980s turned into the 1990s, the expansion of the bookstore chains took a new turn with the advent and spread of book superstores. There had long been a handful of very large bookstores offering an unusually broad, deep selection of titles. An early example was the Barnes & Noble "annex" opened by Len Riggio on New York's Fifth Avenue in 1975, a forty-thousand square-foot store that featured such innovations as grocery-style shopping carts and checkout counters.

Inspired in part by the explosion of superstores in various other retailing categories—from Toys"R"Us and Sports Authority to Home Depot and Staples—other booksellers began experimenting with similar large-format stores. In 1982, entrepreneur Gary Hoover launched the Bookstop chain with a giant store in Austin, Texas; it gradually expanded into locations throughout Texas and Florida. During the late 1970s and the early 1980s, Joyce Meskis steadily expanded the Tattered Cover bookstores in Denver, Colorado, culminating in a move of her flagship store into a vast four-story facility in 1986. And during the 1980s, the Borders chain, which had originated with a single used bookstore in Ann Arbor, Michigan, began opening its own chain of superstores using a unique computerized system designed to select inventory according to the needs and interests of local communities.

All of the giant stores built by these bookselling pioneers could stock 100,000 or more individual book titles as compared with the 20,000 titles typically carried by a mall store. Given the unique nature of the book business, in which tens of thousands of new books are published every year, many of them appealing to small but passionate niche markets of readers, these vast, varied inventories served as powerful magnets for booklovers. A small, nearby mall store might be fine for someone who was interested only in buying the latest bestselling novel. But an avid reader would be willing to drive a few extra miles to visit a store in which she could browse a seemingly endless array of varied titles and perhaps walk away with a shopping bag containing several unexpected discoveries—as well as the ubiquitous bestsellers.

By the end of the 1980s, Len Riggio decided that the future of bookselling, and of Barnes & Noble in particular, lay in superstores. By 1989, B&N was operating twenty-three superstores, and the chain began opening new superstores at a rapid clip—while also gradually shuttering the small mall stores it had opened during the previous decade. By 1992, B&N had 105 superstores; by 1995, 358.

Ingram played a major role in this nationwide bookstore expansion. As we explained in chapter five, Ingram's ROSI program provided in-depth expertise both to bookstore chains and to individual booksellers when planning and executing new-store openings. As B&N built its chain of superstores, the company relied heavily on Ingram's expertise and supply network to establish both their opening inventories and restocking systems. Between 1990 and 1996, Ingram helped manage the opening of around a hundred B&N superstores. This included monitoring sales for the first ninety days of each store's operation, managing stock replenishment as needed, and serving as vendor-of-record for the stores—that is, acting as official inventory manager for the stores in their dealings with publishers.

David Cully, an executive at Barnes & Noble from 1993 to 2000 (and later at Ingram's rival Baker & Taylor), remembers the central role the Ingram team played in B&N's expansion:

> We at Barnes & Noble did not yet have our own distribution
> infrastructure. So we relied on Ingram as an integral part of our

system. They did so much to support our opening of stores. And they were terrific to work with from a logistics standpoint, an inventory management standpoint, a systems standpoint, and from the standpoint of working and partnering with the publishers. There were years when we did over 300 million dollars' worth of business with Ingram. Over time, we developed our own distribution infrastructure, and that infrastructure eventually replaced a lot of the volume that Ingram was doing. But there's no way we could have opened so many stores so quickly without Ingram.

Ingram played a similar role with the other bookstore chains as they continued their rapid growth. These included the independent superstores Davis-Kidd and Joseph-Beth, initially supplied by Borders, which left the Borders network and signed up with Ingram's Bookstore Merchandising program. Regional bookstore chains such as Books-A-Million, Hastings, and Lauriat's also grew during this period, as did such established independents as Tattered Cover, Powell's, BookPeople, and the John Gaylord stores (of Little Professor fame). Ingram provided information, services, and systems in support of all these expansion efforts.

One of the key innovations of this period was Ingram Retailer Systems, which provided point-of-sale software systems that booksellers could use to manage their inventory better. Beginning in 1988, Ingram Retailer Systems was led by Kent Freeman, who you may recall had joined the company in 1982 and had soon been asked to manage the giant IBM mainframe that then was at the heart of Ingram's information systems technology.

This career shift came about at Freeman's own request. He recalls visiting Phil Pfeffer with a request: "I told Phil that I enjoyed what I was doing, but that I felt pretty removed from the actual business. I wanted an opportunity that got me closer to our business while still leveraging my computer background."

Ingram Retailer Systems was that opportunity. "We were really the first to provide electronic ordering applications that changed the way many bookstores operated," Freeman explains. "The bookstore could place an order through their computer terminal and get an immediate response." The introduction of electronic ordering, linking the store instantaneously with current inventory data at Ingram, helped dramatically streamline both sales and customer relations.

Freeman tackled this job with the help of Art Carson, who traveled widely to advise booksellers about how to use this new technology.

"Over the course of the next ten years," Carson recalls, "most independent booksellers implemented one of the top four or five software systems available. They all benefited from the efficiency gains, which included fewer lost sales and increased inventory turns. And of course we liked it when they chose to use the package Ingram recommended, which was called IBID. It had been developed in 1983 by a company out of San Francisco, and it automatically included Ingram's electronic ordering interface. But our main interest was in helping the bookstores become more efficient, no matter which system they picked."

With its deep and growing knowledge of computer systems and information technology, Ingram could provide booksellers with more than just the software they needed. "We could sell you or rent you the PC and the CD drive," Freeman notes. (By this time, the microfiche card, which had been revolutionary in 1972, had been supplemented by CD-ROMs, which had a much greater memory capacity, capable of managing the ever-growing list of book titles that Ingram and its customers needed to track.) "Ingram became one of the leading sellers of CD drives in the country." Thanks in large part to Ingram, more and more independent booksellers were taking big leaps beyond the cash-in-a-cigar-box level of management where many had been stuck.

With its growing array of bookseller services, Ingram helped make the expansion of book retailing in the 1980s and 1990s possible. And, of course, Ingram's own growth was further fueled by the growth of the entire book business.

"During the late 1980s and 1990s," recalls Mike Lovett, who would join Ingram in 1997, "books were a hot entertainment and gift item, and that tide lifted lots of bookstore sales. The publishers' fall lists were always anticipated with excitement." Those fall lists were typically crammed with books by authors with bestselling track records—writers like Stephen King, Tom Clancy, Robert Ludlum, Jackie Collins, Danielle Steel, Garrison Keillor, and Judith Krantz, whose names became brands in their own right.

As a result, Lovett explains,

> Ingram's business was highly seasonal, with peak sales during the fourth-quarter holidays—the gift-giving season. Our five largest sales days of the year were predictably the five Mondays before Christmas. Bookstore sales were mostly on the weekend, and Monday was replenishment ordering day. Books that sold and were reordered would be back on the store shelves for the next weekend, a lovely cycle for everyone."

But rapid business growth generates challenges as well as opportunities. In the fall of 1984, in the aftermath of a major storm in the Nashville area, Ingram was hard-pressed to fulfill customer orders for the ultra-busy Christmas season. Ingram's response to this problem was significant—and typical. "The very next year," Secrest says, "we made plans to expand our operations with two more warehouses, one in Avon, Connecticut, and the other in Fort Wayne, Indiana. That's one of the things that always excited me about Ingram. We always looked for what's next. What's the next opportunity? And how do we prepare our operation to make it work?"

But the pressures continued to grow. In 1989, with the cycle of expansion continuing to accelerate, Ingram's leadership recognized that they were about to face some unprecedented problems. It was a year when Bronson Ingram and Phil Pfeffer had much on their minds. In addition to the book company's dramatic growth, this was also the year Ingram completed its purchase of Micro D, the microcomputer products distributor, and merged it with Ingram Computer. On top of all this, with the critical Christmas selling season approaching, it was clear that Ingram Book was about to have more sales volume than it could handle.

This was not the kind of problem that Pfeffer would let slide. Pfeffer was a driven leader, never one to be satisfied with "good enough" performance. Steve Little remembers reviewing company results with Pfeffer at the end of one particularly successful year. Little expected Pfeffer to be delighted with what the team had accomplished—but instead, he leaned forward, pointed to the others around the table, and declared, "I'll never be satisfied until the day we have zero inventory and a 100 percent fill rate!"

No wonder Little also says, "Some of us would refer to Phil as 'Mr. Good . . . But' because he loved to tell us, 'What you've done is really good, but . . . '" During a skit at one Christmas party, Phil was even ceremoniously presented with a "Mr. Good But" candy bar in a package designed to resemble the Hershey's Mr. Goodbar wrapper.

So for Pfeffer—as well as for Bronson—the possibility of having the warehousing system overwhelmed by excessive demand was not acceptable. They determined it was time to inject some new leadership into the La Vergne front office.

Pfeffer was also, at heart, a financial and logistics manager. He proposed recruiting a manager who could navigate the book company through a period of turbulent growth. Pfeffer himself would remain a prominent part of the leadership mix as executive vice president of Ingram Industries, with particular accountability for the book company. But adding a new leader to tackle the daily problems of the book business would allow Pfeffer to devote more time and energy to the rapidly evolving software business, which had many challenges of its own.

* * *

In 1989, Lee Synnott became the chairman and CEO of the book company. A native of Port Arthur, Texas, he came to Ingram from Maremont Corporation, a leader in the automotive parts supply industry. To outsiders, this might have seemed an unlikely hire. But in fact books and auto parts, at the wholesale supply level, have a number of surprising similarities. Synnott explains:

> I had spent a lot of years in the automotive industry, which is about lots and lots of stock keeping units—SKUs. And they have to be quickly available to the consumer, because the consumer has to have his car ready to go. The whole of that industry is geared to provide prescription parts to a mechanic's bay, maybe the same day. Millions of parts. Very similar to the book industry. I'd spent years in distribution, and was for fifteen years a leader in the information technology world. Maremont used that as a competitive edge. And at the time that I joined the book industry, the average price point in the auto parts business, believe it or not, was about the same as in books. So the two businesses actually had a lot in common.

Synnott had already met several Ingram-connected people during his master's degree program at Vanderbilt's Owen Graduate School of Management. One was the dean, Sam Richmond, who was a member of the Ingram Industries board of directors. Also, Michael Head, Ingram Industries' human resources director, had been a classmate at the business school.

Synnott remembers the interview process for his new role at Ingram as careful and long, stretching over three or four months in late 1989. When the search ended and the executives settled on Synnott, he was careful to establish clear communications with Pfeffer.

"Of course, the book business was Phil's baby," Synnott recalls.

> Intellectually, he loved handing it off and teaching me about the book business, so he was sort of like a parent who was maybe going to give up his child—he was protective of it. But we had a great relationship, offices adjacent to one another. I spent a lot of time with him, and we saw eye-to-eye on many things.
>
> The thing that I told Phil at the outset was, "You have to tell me the rules, and then you have to let me have my head. I'm really good at this distribution stuff, and I've been doing it a long time." And while the

computer business was gangbusters and '89 was a record year, the book business couldn't serve its customers in the 1989 season. We stubbed our toe, and badly. During that Christmas season, we had to tell our customers, "If you want your books for the holidays, you better go someplace else to get them. Because we've got a huge backlog." That had never happened before.

The problem was a combination of shipping troubles because of increased volume and an imbalance among stock held at Ingram's three distribution centers. The warehouse at Jessup, Maryland, had the largest inventory at some 60,000 titles. By contrast, La Vergne had about 35,000, and the facility at City of Industry, California, held some 20,000. "So the mother lode was at Jessup, which was close to most of the publishers," Synnott explains. "And we measured our fill rate at that time based on what we intended to ship, not what the customer ordered. Big difference."

When Synnott took over following the end of the difficult 1989 holiday season, he made some immediate changes. One was to assemble his own senior staff, principally from among longtime Ingram leaders. He moved seven executives into the new C-suite.

Ray Taylor, who had been responsible for distribution for the book company and had been one of the key players who put the early systems architecture in place, had left Ingram to get into the video rentailing business. Synnott, with Pfeffer's concurrence, now invited Taylor back. Lavona Russell became Taylor's second-in-command, and later she would become president of Ingram Book.

Buddy Pickler, another early book company leader who had also moved to the video business, was brought back in to better tune up the systems architecture, including software support.

Steven Mason, the attorney who had served as president of the book company, became vice chairman with responsibilities for Ingram Library Services as well.

Others in the new leadership array were Ron Hardaway as vice president for finance; Steve Little, vice president for product; and Larry Carpenter, who had reported to Little, as vice president for marketing.

Over the next seven years, the Synnott team would record many accomplishments. In 1991, Ingram acquired the regional Denver-based wholesaler Gordon's Books. Then, over time, a network of new distribution centers was opened. The Avon, Connecticut, distribution center was moved to East Windsor in 1995. Two existing distribution centers were moved to new locations: operations in Maryland, at Jessup, were shifted to Petersburg, Virginia, and California operations, at City of Industry, were moved to Chino.

The effect of all these moves was to redeploy Ingram's main customer-facing activities, moving them strategically closer to the growing customer base. The company could now, more confidently promise next-day deliveries on most books to most bookstores and, in the more distant reaches, two-day or, at most, three-day deliveries. This made Ingram unique in the industry. Only Ingram could deliver book orders so quickly and accurately to almost anywhere in the continental United States.

Lovett remembers Pfeffer calling this period the "golden age of Ingram Book Company." The company's success during the first half of the 1990s was the culmination of the hard work by the many folks who had put Ingram on the map over the previous twenty years. Lovett views this "golden age" as reflecting an economic business model he considers close to ideal. "From my view, the book industry in those days really captured the Adam Smith model of free market competition," Lovett says. "It was a business with lots of suppliers (publishers) and lots of customers (bookstores) all competing to serve and satisfy each other. Ingram had a great position between the two, with products and information flowing through Ingram."

Ingram capitalized on this privileged position by continuing to create programs that benefited its customers. One was the Ingram Platinum Publisher Partner program, developed and promoted by Little. "Being a member of this program was a cherished honor," Lovett says, "which had to be earned with favorable trading terms. In return, Publisher Partners had access to information they couldn't get anywhere else, along with other benefits. We also carried many more titles in stock than anyone else, including through our Greenlight program. This benefited both publishers, who could get their products into the hands of more readers, and the booksellers, who were able to offer an even wider array of goods to their customers."

By the mid-1990s, Ingram had developed divisions offering specialized services to particular categories of customers—in particular, to libraries and to international booksellers. These divisions were placed under the leadership of Lovett.

Supplying books to both academic and public libraries had been part of Ingram's portfolio of services since the company's earliest days. But this function lacked scale, and the competition was strong. (The leaders in this field were Baker & Taylor, followed by Brodart, with Ingram a distant number three.) Lovett sought to strengthen Ingram's activities in this field by creating a division called Ingram Library Services.

"The first item on the agenda was to build our leadership team," Lovett recalls.

> Larry Price, a former library director, was our library leader, but after him we were thin. To beef up, we hired more library experts, including Wendell Lotz, Rebecca James, Shannon McGuire, and Stephanie Lanzalotto. Some of these had formerly worked for Baker & Taylor. Others had been librarians themselves—in fact, by the end of 1996, Ingram Library had approximately twenty librarians on its staff.
>
> Our goal was to become a full-service library provider, with expert cataloging and processing capabilities and library system interfaces. Our new team traveled across the country in the Ingram jet, a Cessna Citation VI, to meet with representatives of the major library system vendors—software companies that provide library management tools to libraries.
>
> To help us establish a market presence, prove our capabilities, and build the Ingram Library Services brand, we wanted to win a marquee account. Thanks to Larry and Rebecca, we became the primary supplier to the Chicago Public Library, knocking out B&T. This was the largest public library in the world, with about fifteen million volumes in its collection and eighty-two branches at the time—a larger account than many of the major bookstore chains.

A second front that Lovett focused on was international sales. Previously, book exports had not been a high priority for Ingram, and sales figures showed it. The Ingram International division lacked some essential systems interfaces and basic expertise regarding international business, as illustrated by an incident from 1995. At the time, before the widespread adoption of e-mail, about 20 percent of the international orders Ingram received arrived via fax machine. One Monday morning, a staff member noted that the office had not received many foreign orders over the weekend. Then someone else observed that the fax machine was always out of paper on Monday morning. They put two and two together and realized that many orders had simply been lost because they'd never been printed out. Two new fax machines with rollover capability were installed in the office, leading to a noticeable increase in monthly sales.

In the mid-1990s, the international business began to show improved results. Ingram began flying shipments of books direct from Nashville to the United Kingdom once or twice a week. From London, the books would get distributed by European postal services throughout the continent. This was a lucrative business for Ingram, in part because US books were sold at a premium in Europe. Ingram International staff members became regular participants in the annual Frankfurt and London book fairs, and new relationships with publishers and retailers were developed in Japan (Maruzen, Tower), Germany (Libri), the United Kingdom (Blackwell), and Canada (Chapters, Indigo).

In September 1997, Lovett became the CEO of Ingram Book. He would serve in this position for seven years.

* * *

THE BOOK BUSINESS HAD EXPERIENCED two decades of seismic change. The fragmented sales and distribution system, plagued by inefficiency, delays, and data gaps, had given way to a world in which information about books—and books themselves—could be delivered across the country and even around the globe with unprecedented speed. America's old-fashioned book trade, made up mainly of small stores with spotty inventory run by lovers of literature with little understanding of or interest in business management, was being replaced by networks of book superstores boasting vast numbers of titles that could be replenished quickly and easily based on customer demand. Partly as a result of these changes, books attained new heights of preeminence in popular culture, evidenced not only by the explosion of brand-name authors whose books were virtually guaranteed bestsellers, but also by phenomena like Oprah's Book Club, launched by the talk show host in 1996, which routinely transformed little-known authors into multimedia celebrities.

The new book publishing landscape would have astonished any observer who'd last surveyed the field a generation earlier. And none of these changes would have been possible without the innovations pioneered by a company whose name was known to just a tiny fraction of the millions of booklovers who relied on it—Ingram.

10

CONSOLIDATION AND NEW CHALLENGES

The era of dramatic changes to the book business continued in the late 1990s. In particular, it was a period of consolidation. The thousands of small, independent economic units on both sides of the book market began to combine and shrink in number, altering the landscape for both groups as well as for their leading intermediary, the national wholesaler Ingram.

On the publisher side, during the 1980s and 1990s, the number of leading book publishing houses shrank, continuing a process that had begun in the 1960s. In particular, the Big Six US publishers grew bigger through acquisitions of smaller companies. Among other notable deals, Simon & Schuster bought Prentice Hall (1985); Random House bought Crown Publishers (1988); and Penguin bought Putnam Berkley (1996). (The Big Six would become the Big Five in 2013 with the acquisition of Penguin by Random House.)

Diversified media corporations had already become major forces in US book publishing through moves like Time Inc.'s purchase of Little, Brown (1968) and Gulf & Western's purchase of Simon & Schuster (1976). Now the media giants expanded their footprints in the industry. For example, Rupert Murdoch's News Corporation bought the venerable US firm of Harper & Row (1987), then the British publisher William Collins, Sons (1989), producing a new giant known as HarperCollins. Other European-based firms became major presences in US book publishing with the sale of Random House to the German Bertelsmann (1998) and the sale of Macmillan, first to the UK firm of Pearson (1998), then to the German Holtzbrinck (2001).

By the end of this period, US book publishing continued to be one of the nation's more fragmented industries (compared with, for example, auto manufacturing), but it had taken several large steps in the direction of consolidation.

On the retail side, the spread of superstores during the 1990s—especially those being opened by the Barnes & Noble chain—exerted increasingly competitive pressures on smaller booksellers. Neighborhood bookstores, even ones that had been in business for generations, found it hard to retain their customers when a giant new superstore opened nearby. Boasting seemingly unlimited inventory and often attractively discounted prices, especially on bestsellers, as well as amenities like in-store coffee shops, the superstores were hard to beat. Even specialized bookstores known for their unique product knowledge found the superstore competition daunting. For example, the nationwide network of Christian bookstores, which had experienced its own phenomenal growth spurt during the 1980s, began to wither during the 1990s as customers realized that most of the religiously oriented books they wanted could be found on the shelves of the nearest Barnes & Noble or Borders.

As a result, independent bookstores gradually began to close. The American Booksellers Association, the trade group that advocates particularly for the independents, saw its membership decline over the decade, from 5,200 bookstores in 1991 to 3,300 in 1998. By 2002, the number of ABA member stores would decline even further to 2,191.

Thus, the bookstore market share became increasingly concentrated in large chains. As a result, the share of Ingram sales represented by independent stores shrank from more than half to less than 15 percent during this period.

The rise of B&N and the decline of independent bookstores became sources of widespread controversy. Publishers, authors, booklovers, and others concerned with the health and diversity of American literary culture worried about the replacement of thousands of independent bookstores by a seemingly monolithic chain of superstores that, as critics complained, merchandised books in the same way that McDonald's sold hamburgers.

During these years of conflict, Ingram executives sought to maintain their own company's neutrality. They repeated the slogan, "Ingram is Switzerland," reminding their associates that it was never Ingram's place as a wholesaler to take sides.

But Ingram itself came under pressure as a result of the industry's advancing consolidation. As the giant bookstore chains continued their growth, B&N, Borders, and others began establishing dedicated regional distribution centers of their own. This enabled the chains to buy directly from publishers at prices as advantageous as those provided to wholesalers. They could likewise implement efficient scheduled delivery systems to their stores. Thus, Ingram's important role in the book business began to be challenged, demanding still more adaptive change from Ingram.

And from another corner, yet another seismic change was in the works that would revolutionize the book business. This one was spurred by a business innovator named Jeff Bezos. That is a complex story we'll delve into in a later chapter.

* * *

IN THE TURBULENT BUSINESS AND technology world of the late 1980s and early 1990s, not all of the initiatives launched by Ingram proved to be successful. However, even those that faltered helped the company develop capabilities that would later reemerge in different and highly successful forms.

Ingram's Publisher Resources Inc. (PRI) was created in the late 1980s. Its purpose was to offer contract distribution services for publishing partners who needed such support, including such well-known publishers as Boston-based Houghton Mifflin. However, PRI was designed as a separate business rather than being fully integrated into the mainline Ingram system. The name "Ingram" didn't even appear on any of the packaging used by the company on its shipments to customers. This served the needs of some publishers, who were uncomfortable with having Ingram appear as the face of their businesses. But the systemic separation of PRI from the Ingram mainstream gradually came to be seen as a flawed business model, since building a new distribution system with its own independent processes was both difficult and costly. Furthermore, since PRI did not bring its publisher customers sufficient value-adding services, it was seen as representing a cost-item for publishers rather than a source of added value.

Over time, PRI was gradually dismantled, and ceased operations by 2003. Within a year, a new approach to distribution services was launched under the name of Ingram Publisher Services. Tightly integrated into the main Ingram structure and, over time, offering massive, valuable digital services in support of its publisher customers, Ingram Publisher Services provided the kind of value PRI had failed to create, and it grew quickly into an important part of the Ingram array of offerings.

Another service offering whose initial form proved unsuccessful was Ingram Internet Support Services, known internally by its high-tech acronym I^2S^2. Launched with strong support from John Ingram in 1996, I^2S^2 was the company's first attempt to launch an Internet-based bookselling operation. It had become clear that Amazon's online bookselling model was working, sending ripples of concern through Ingram's community of traditional booksellers. The idea behind I^2S^2 was that Ingram would create an online sales platform for brick-and-mortar booksellers, handling shipping to customers direct from Ingram's warehouses but with the bookseller's name and return address on the packages.

Unfortunately, I^2S^2 never made much headway, and it was abandoned in less than a year. One reason may have been Amazon's decision, around the same time, to adopt an aggressive discounting policy on almost all of the books it sold, which put Ingram's potential online bookselling partners in a terrible bind. Trying to match Amazon's pricing by cutting 30 to 35 percent off the recommended retail price of a book would shave the booksellers' already thin profit margins to the bone. And given the incredible ease of Internet surfing, with Amazon's low price always a click away, trying to sell books at a higher price than Amazon would have been a futile effort.

However, John looks back on the failure of I²S² with equanimity. "Launching I²S² forced us to create a deadline for developing a workable system for third-party distribution and sales," he says. The ability to ship products directly to consumers on behalf of retailers has since grown into a powerful capability, representing a sizeable fraction of Ingram's business. The I²S² project also helped prepare Ingram for other initiatives in Internet-based marketing, notably its ground-breaking iPage merchandising platform for booksellers.

Through all these dramatic industry shifts, Ingram continued to play a crucial role—driving some of the most important changes itself, while in other cases creating brilliant service, information, and systems innovations that would enable thousands of industry players to adapt to the changes efficiently and profitably.

Jack Romanos had a long and storied career in book publishing, beginning in the 1970s with a stint as director of sales for Bantam Books, then the nation's largest mass-market publisher. Romanos eventually rose to become president and CEO of Simon & Schuster. Having personally navigated many of the twists and turns in the book trade's complicated history, Romanos provides a long view of Ingram's place in an ever-transitioning industry.

"If you look at the last fifty years of trade publishing in America," Romanos says, "Ingram's evolution is as important as anything that's happened. They were a classy organization and great to work with—true partners in the publishing process, which is not something I could always say for others. They understood that they needed us just as much as we needed them, which was the basis for a very strong and positive relationship between Ingram and the rest of our industry. I wouldn't have wanted to have to run a great publishing company without Ingram's help and support."

As the final years of the twentieth century ticked down, the rate of change in the publishing business—and in other industries of virtually every kind—showed little sign of slowing. In particular, the digital revolution that had been launched by innovators like Microsoft and Apple in the 1980s was now rapidly transforming the worlds of marketing, sales, and media. It meant that Ingram's leadership needed to be ready to weather yet another period of unpredictable change—and, if possible, to play a leadership role in shaping it.

*In this file photo from the 1947 christening of the towboat E.B. Ingram the honoree
Erskine Bronson Ingram is seated on deck. His son Orrin Henry Ingram,
standing at right, had named the boat for his father.
Also shown are the boat's captain and a company executive.*

*Orrin Henry (Hank) Ingram, the
grandfather of John R. Ingram,
brought his new bride Hortense to
Nashville from St. Paul, Minnesota,
in 1928.*

E. Bronson Ingram and Jack Stambaugh acquired Tennessee School Book Depository in 1964, making it part of the Ingram family of businesses. The name was changed to Tennessee Book Company. In 1970 it was renamed Ingram Book Company.

John (Jack) H. Stambaugh was Vanderbilt University's Vice Chancellor for Business Affairs from 1956 to 1962. There he met Hank Ingram and later his son Bronson.

Harry Hoffman was the first president of Ingram Book Company. After building the business, he left in 1979 to become CEO of Waldenbooks.

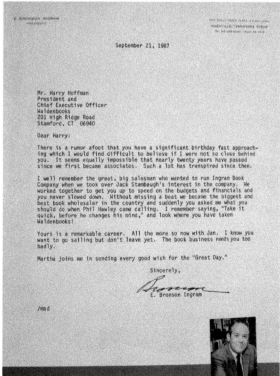

In 1987, Bronson Ingram sent Hoffman best wishes on his birthday.

Tom Clarkson (shown here during a 2018 interview) was hired by Hoffman to modernize computer systems in the early years of the book company. This became the backbone of Ingram's ordering processes for booksellers and libraries.

Michael Zibart, center, was hired by Hoffman to coordinate sales. With him in this early staff photo are (left to right): Carol Wetherington Halloway, Sue Kinack, Kiki Davis, Patti Pigg, the credit manager Suzanne Close, Helen Hawkins, Anne Svoboda Phifer, and Susan Walker Nathan.

Philip M. Pfeffer, right, was named president of Ingram Book in 1979. This opened a period of dramatic growth, as well as diversification of products and creation of Ingram Distribution Group, which Pfeffer ran. Steven Mason, left, then became president of the book company.

Kent Freeman joined Ingram in June of 1982. With Tom Clarkson and others, he was an early designer of the company's data processing architecture. He is now the president of Ingram's VitalSource Technologies.

Art Carson came to Ingram with the acquisition of the West Coast distributor Raymar. Zibart hired Carson to be Ingram's first marketing director.

The Ingram family on a 1980 vacation at Sea Island, Georgia. From left to right are David, Orrin III, Bronson, Robin, John, and Martha.

*When David Ingram worked summers in the Book Company
warehouse, he came up with this invention for more
efficiently packing books of different sizes for shipment.*

*When Ingram relocated to its new headquarters in La Vergne in 1985, Willie Collins,
left, supervisor in the telephone sales department, celebrated the move with her boss
Carol McElwain, right. (The writing was on the snapshot, not the wall.)*

*Joani Lehman, left, Art Carson, center, and Lavona Russell
(talking with a customer, at right) were among the Ingram associates
who staffed the Ingram booth at an early book industry trade show.*

*Mike Zibart, kneeling, with early Ingram sales team members (left to right):
Sarah Benson, Joani Lehman, Debbie Presnell, Anne Mogensen,
Lucy Wright, Jim Parker, Kathy Fleming, Theresa Shackelford,
Cathey Clark, Ingrid Fidler, Pat Sadler, and Sara Fortenberry.*

Steven Mason, center, then-president of Ingram Book, celebrates with the company's winning 1985 softball team with (left to right): Nancy Smith, Tanya Vaughn, Regina Rose, Billie Cunningham, Phillip Minter, Russell Knight, Cherie Gigandet, Sandy Smith, Vera Thompson, Emily Leach, Terry Baker, Kim Gipson, Cindy Neil, and Darlene Sullivan.

Lee Synnott, center, presides at a service award reception with Carol McElwain, left, and Janet Hill, right.

Industry trade shows became an important venue for meeting customers and introducing innovations. Here, the Ingram booth in 1998 at BookExpo America. BEA became the industry's largest in the United States.

LIGHTNING PRINT AND "*i* PAGE" ARE 'BIG HITS' AT BOOK EXPO AMERICA

Lightning Print Inc. (LPI) and Ingram Customer Systems' "*i* Page" program made a dazzling debut with the book industry at the 1998 BookExpo America.

BookExpo America (BEA) is an annual show for booksellers, book publishers and distributors. This year's BEA was held in Chicago on the weekend of May 30 through June 1.

"One of the show's big

college store markets because of their frequent access to the Internet, but general retail markets have been very receptive," Neal said.

Ingram Customer Systems' "*i* Page" is a web-based information, title selection and stock inquiry tool that enables retail booksellers and librarians

attention-getters was the display of on-demand printing technology. Ingram's Lightning Print operation had a printer near the autographing area that created finished books while you waited. The entire process, from blank paper to finished bound book, took no more than a minute." — *Publishers Weekly*

Lightning Print's display was a demonstration of the book production line at Lightning Print in La Vergne, Tennessee. IBM and Danka Services International, which are in an alliance with Ingram to provide the technology for LPI, also worked in Lightning Print's display area to assist visitors. IBM associates took two days to construct and two days to take down the eye-catching display. Lightning Print produced sample books throughout the show.

"I think visitors to LPI's display were thoroughly impressed," Jeanne Pollock, Marketing Manager for Lightning Print, said. "They were amazed at the speed, the beautiful quality and the pricing for the Lightning Print books," Jeanne added.

"Our "*i* Page" display stayed extremely busy," Neal Webb, of Ingram Customer Systems, said. "We set up 20 computers and performed nearly 1,000 demonstrations of the web-site. We left BEA with close to 150 new "*i* Page" users, and we're receiving new subscriptions daily since the show.

"We knew that "*i* Page" would be a big hit with library and

to find large amounts of information about specific book titles, categories and the book industry to help better serve their customers. Booksellers and librarians who are Ingram customers have access to "*i* Page" through the Internet.

Ingram companies attending this year's BEA included Ingram International, Lightning Print, Ingram Library Services, Ingram Periodicals, Customer Systems, Integra Design Group (Spring Arbor division), White Bridge Communications and Publisher Resources Inc.

This page from the company's newsletter featured scenes of Ingram associates on the job at BookExpo America in 1998, where Lightning's "print on demand" technology was unveiled.

Mike Lovett, formerly the chief financial officer,
was named CEO of Ingram Book Group in 1997.
He served in that role until his retirement in 2004.

John Ingram, right, greets publisher Larry Kirschbaum, left,
and literary agent Bob DiForio, center, at the Ingram booth
during the 2011 BookExpo in New York City.

Members of Ingram's telephone sales staff in 1984. Shown here are Laura Delay, Candace Walden, Janet Hill, John O'Day, Lisa Phillips, Kim Smith, Sharon Goar, Lee Winsett, Diane Pysz, Karen Lasher, Diane Tummons, Cathy Merritt, Ann Carson, Serena Wright, Tanya Eakes, Willie Collins, and Lynn Trigg.

Author Margaret Atwood brought star power to Ingram's booth at BookExpo in 2011.

Printing Impressions *magazine featured three leaders of Lightning Source on its March 2007 cover. Left to right, Charles Marshall, J. Kirby Best, and David Taylor.*

Martha Ingram and Youngsuk ('YS') Chi in 2013, when John Ingram was honored by the publishing division of the United Jewish Appeal in New York City. Chi became a member of the Ingram Industries board of directors in 2018.

"Ingramus Prime," above, appeared at the Ingram sales conference in 2013. At right, "Ingramus Prime" removes his helmet to reveal John Ingram.

Phil Ollila, Ingram's chief content officer. He came to the company in 2004 and designed the Ingram Publisher Services business.

*Mike Lovett, center, speaks to associates at the retirement reception
for Sharon Fields in 2009.*

*Frank Kerrigan was the longtime chief financial officer
for Ingram Content Group.*

Shawn Morin, right, joined Ingram in 2009 as chief technology officer.
He became president and chief operating officer of the company in 2016.
In this 2019 photo, he joins John Ingram at a gathering of Ingram associates.

Martha Ingram and the Ingram family have contributed to
the growth of Nashville, especially in the performing arts.
Here, she visits with Nashville's Mayor David Briley in 2018.

*Orrin H. Ingram III, right, president and CEO of Ingram Industries and
CEO of the Barge Company, greets Congressman Jim Cooper, left,
and Aubrey Harwell, center, member of the Ingram board,
at a towboat christening in 2016.*

PART THREE
The Disruption

11

The Rise of an Intrapreneur

On the night that John Ingram learned his father, Bronson, was dying, an ocean and parts of two continents lay between him and home. He was working in Europe at the time, and on this particular Friday evening in early December 1994, he was on holiday in the Austrian high country, far removed from his Nashville family.

It was around eight o'clock when the call came. Sitting with John at a dinner table in a hotel bar in Sölden were three other men. Roland Richter and Koen Philipson were executives of Novell, a big manufacturer of computer networking systems and an important vendor to Ingram Micro.

The third man at the table was Youngsuk (YS) Chi, John's close friend since their undergraduate days at Princeton. They had met in John's dormitory room on the evening in 1980 when a crowd of students had gathered around John's TV to watch the much-anticipated episode of *Dallas*, in which the mystery of "Who shot J.R.?" would be solved. Now, fourteen years and a Columbia MBA later, YS was John's fellow executive in Ingram Micro Europe.

The day had been long but enjoyable. Novell had hosted a day of skiing on the sun-washed slopes of the Austrian Tyrol, and now dinner. "It had been a glorious, sunny day," Chi remembers. "It was just one of those days when everything was right. We came from Munich, because we had business in Munich, with Ingram Micro Germany. I remember getting there from Munich was a pain, because we had some weather problem—we rented a car in Munich, and John and I just drove from Munich to Austria, about two hours away—but once we got there, it was glorious."

Then a young woman in a hotel uniform walked over to their table.

"Is there a John Ingram here?" she asked.

"That's me," John answered.

"You have a phone call," she said, and pointed to the hotel lobby.

John quickly excused himself and walked to the reception desk. He saw the waiting phone and picked it up. Then he heard his mother's voice.

"John, we just heard the news from the doctor," she said. "Your father's really sick. He's got cancer throughout his body, and he wants you to come home."

"I'm so sorry," was all John could say. "I'll be on a flight home as soon as I can."

John had last seen his father some ten days earlier, over the Thanksgiving weekend, in Charleston, South Carolina, Martha's hometown. The extended Ingram family—Bronson, Martha, and their four adult children with their own young families—would traditionally gather for that holiday weekend each November. By then, Bronson had been visibly ill.

"When I saw my father, he didn't look well," John recalls, "and he wasn't feeling well. He had pain in his back and his neck, and bumps on his head."

John also remembered, fondly, the last business discussion he and his father had shared on a gray afternoon in Scotland, near the St. Andrews golf course:

> I had flown to Scotland to a publisher conference. It was a cold, rainy day, probably in October 1994. Dad and I had talked about my staying in Europe for a total of two years, which was almost up. I phoned him and said, "Dad, I know we talked about my leaving Europe soon. But things are looking up, and I hate to step away just now."
>
> He said okay. But all that changed six weeks later.

Returning now to the dinner table in the hotel bar, John kept this news to himself. He did not share what he had learned with his two dinner hosts, nor even with his old friend YS—not until later, after dinner, when they were alone.

"We did not know what had happened," Chi remembers. "When John returned to the table, I just asked him, 'What was the call about?' He looked at me and he said, 'We'll talk afterward.'" After dinner, once on the small hotel elevator, they exchanged these words:

"You know that pain he had?" John said.

"Yes," Chi replied. "He said it was uncomfortable, and it was bothering his golf game."

"It's cancer," John said.

John told no one else of his father's illness, not until Monday. That was the soonest he could speak privately with his own boss, John Winkelhaus, Ingram Micro's president for Europe. "John, I have to go home and see what the hell is going on," he said. That evening, John packed his suitcase, and the next morning he began a long, solitary journey home.

Once on the ground in Nashville, John visited with his father, mother, and siblings. From these long conversations, it quickly became clear that John's immediate future was no longer in Brussels, Munich, or anywhere else in Europe.

"It didn't take long to figure out that I was moving home," John remembers, "because Dad was really sick. I moved home by Christmas, and I started in January as head of sales for Ingram Book Company."

* * *

JOHN'S TIME IN EUROPE WITH Ingram Micro had proved to be a formative period for him as a businessman.

Like his brothers Orrin and David, John had spent parts of his summers working in the family business, often doing entry-level jobs like picking products to fill orders in the Reedwood Drive distribution center. It happened that one summer, John worked in what was then known as the "computer department," a tiny operation made up of just two people. Then, in 1986, after receiving his MBA from Vanderbilt's Owen Graduate School of Management, John became assistant to the treasurer of Ingram Industries—a good training ground because, as John observes, "treasury is one of the core areas that sees everything."

In 1989, Bronson asked John to take over the job of managing the Tennessee Book Company, a textbook distributor that was the direct descendant of the small company that had launched Ingram into the book business in the first place. For years, it had been a self-contained operation separate from the main Ingram Book Company. In fact, it was run for four decades by a man named Herschel Gaddis, who kept a vast storehouse of company procedures purely in his head, making it hard for anyone else to understand how the business worked. What's more, little had been done to keep the Tennessee Book Company up to date with the strategic and technological improvements made throughout the rest of the Ingram businesses. Over time, the disconnect had become a real problem. As John himself remarked at the time, "We're just hanging off the back of the Ingram Book Company system. It's like water skiing behind an aircraft carrier."

Investigating, John found that the Tennessee Book Company's information technology systems were badly outdated. "Because our handling of data was so backward," John recalls, "things that were really dysfunctional were happening—like having to wait for payment on a multimillion-dollar order by one of our biggest customers until one free teacher's edition was delivered."

To fix the problem, John hired a systems integration expert named Charles Marshall, who transformed the company's IT systems. This and other well-conceived moves brought the Tennessee Book Company into the modern world, enabling it to be far more efficient and profitable than ever before.

In 1991, John left the book company to become a director of purchasing for the microcomputer products division, now known as Ingram Micro and headed by Chip Lacy. He moved to Corona del Mar in southern California, near Santa Ana, where the operation was based. "It was almost like working for a non-Ingram company," John recalls, "because we still had a strong feeling of the old Micro D culture. I had a team of buyers working for me, buying software, accessories, and all kinds of other products that didn't fit neatly into any category. We jokingly called it Junk D."

After two years, John was asked to move to Europe, where Ingram Micro was then expanding its operations, chiefly through acquisitions. The growth opportunities were enormous.

> Most of the small distributors that we bought in Europe only represented one or two lines of business. But Ingram had relationships with Microsoft, Lotus, Borland, Ashton-Tate—all the biggest US software companies at that time," John recalls. "In fact, Ingram Micro was the single largest customer for some of these companies, which gave us a lot of leverage. So whenever we started operations in a particular European country—let's say Belgium—we could offer a broad line of products, which meant we could double or even quadruple the volume of business those distributors had been doing.

But John soon realized that Ingram Micro faced some big issues in making the most of its European opportunities. "At the time," he explains, "every country in Europe did business separately, in its own currency—francs in Belgium, guilders in Holland, marks in Germany, and so on." (The euro was not generally adopted as the official currency of the European Union until 2002.) "This created financial risk as the relative values of these currencies were continually fluctuating." And that was just the start of the challenges. John explains:

> In addition, thanks in part to the cultural frictions that existed between countries, Europe was made up of a series of small, separate, fragmented markets. That created a management problem for us. The Ingram Micro systems for finance and information management were fine for a big country like the United States, but not so much for the small countries in Europe. The back end of our operations was pretty labor intensive in those days, so setting up a separate management system in every little country meant there was a huge amount of

duplication of effort, which was inefficient and expensive. As a result, we were losing a ton of money over there, despite the fact that our sales volume was strong.

The Ingram team of which John was a part set about solving these problems. They began building a European operation that sold multiple product lines and was organized on regional rather than national lines. They consolidated operations where they could while retaining nationally based offices where they were needed. "For cultural reasons, sales and marketing are always local," John explains. "But functions like accounting, information systems, and logistics don't need to be. Regionalizing them allowed us to take advantage of scale and create significant financial leverage." This was a more-difficult version of the transitions that Ingram had successfully managed in the United States—building the first nationwide book wholesaler, and later becoming the first nationwide distributor of video and game products and microcomputer software, hardware, and accessories.

Ingram Micro set about building its first regional warehouse in Lille, France. It was designed to serve not just France but also Belgium and Holland. At the same time, the company was struggling to build a European management team that could oversee operations across the continent—while also dealing with the local, nationally based teams that were still considered to be essential. In the process, John developed a deep awareness of the cultural differences that made business in Europe challenging:

> As we built our European business, we had John Winkelhaus, an American, running it. And as we worked and talked with our European partners, we discovered that they were fine with an American manager. But they would have been very leery of a German running it, or even a Brit or a Frenchman. It was all about history, and the centuries of conflict among the big powers of Europe. If we had to install a European to run our headquarters in Brussels, the people over there would have been much more comfortable with a Dutch or Swiss leader—someone from one of the small, neutral countries that no one found threatening.

The leadership challenge became very personal for John after he'd been in Europe for just two months. One day, his boss Chip Lacy came into his office, plopped into a chair, and asked, "John, how's your Dutch?"

Puzzled, John replied, "I don't speak Dutch."

"That's okay," Chip said. "Everybody in Holland speaks English anyway. I've got to fire the managing director of our operation in Holland. I want you to take over."

The Dutch headquarters was just about 170 kilometers (105 miles) from Brussels, where John was then based. "But in terms of culture, they seemed about a million miles apart," John says. He quickly realized that the operation in Holland had not been well-managed. He started working twelve-hour days, traveling back and forth between Brussels and Utrecht while working desperately hard to clean up the mess he'd inherited. "It's a good thing I wasn't married at the time," John recalls, "because I was super busy. It was really a tough assignment, and I knew I had to make it work somehow. To have to return to the United States without having succeeded in Europe would not have been very good."

He recalls an exchange with the accountant Anne-Marie Topps, who was essentially the head of finance for Ingram Micro in Holland, during a planning meeting.

"John, you're an Ingram. You can't fail," Topps said.

"Well, that's really the point of the matter, isn't it?" John responded. "I sure as hell can fail. I just don't want to."

In the midst of these struggles, John encountered Erik van Netten, founder and CEO of Trend Group, which was the largest distributor of HP printers in Holland. John discovered that Trend was well-run and had an excellent management team. He set about convincing van Netten to sell his company to Ingram—mainly in order to take advantage of van Netten's own management skills.

John remembers having to convince his father, Bronson, to approve the acquisition.

"Dad asked, 'Why do we have to pay a premium price for this Dutch company you want to buy?' I told him, 'Because it's a great business—not like the challenged companies we've been buying everywhere else!'"

Bronson gave his okay, and Ingram made the deal. Van Netten and his team took over Ingram's Dutch operation, and it turned into the best-performing Ingram company in all of Europe for the next few years.

John himself then returned full-time to Brussels, where he ran the central purchasing operation for Ingram Micro. He was responsible for trying to harmonize the company's purchasing practices across a dozen countries—no easy feat. In the end, Ingram Micro became the leading distributor of computer software and hardware in Europe. And for John Ingram, his stint with Ingram Micro—first in California, then in Europe—was a formative experience. He'd stared down the real possibility of failure, and survived. Years later, when faced with any tough challenge, John would say to himself, "Well, this may be hard, but it's not as hard as what I had to do in Europe."

Ultimately, in 1996, the Ingram family took Ingram Micro public again. The initial public offering of Ingram Micro stock became a singular source of new wealth not only for the family members but for many Ingram associates, including retirees through the Ingram 401(k) matching funds program.

This, then, was the formative career stint that had done so much to shape John Ingram's gut-level sense about how the business world works. Now he was about to begin learning whether he'd been adequately prepared to try to fill his father's enormous shoes.

* * *

WHEN BRONSON INGRAM DIED ON June 15, 1995, he was only sixty-three years old. "He was at the peak of his powers," his friend the Nashville banker Kenneth L. Roberts observed at the time.

From the time of his cancer diagnosis until his death, the Ingram family and front office sought, in at least two internal memoranda, to assure all Ingram associates that the businesses were in good operational shape, under well-known management, and would continue to be so. On December 6, 1994, Bronson wrote the first message about his diagnosis, a letter that Chip Lacy distributed to thirty-three senior officers of Ingram Industries and its subsidiary units. It read, it part:

> As many of you know, I have been having some lower back pain and neck discomfort and in the last few weeks have developed some lumps on my head. Results of a biopsy determined last Friday that these were malignant and extensive CAT scans yesterday confirmed that the back and neck were more of the same.
>
> I have spent today at Vanderbilt determining a course of action that will begin with radiation therapy on the back and neck to be followed by chemotherapy . . .
>
> I wanted you to know of my condition before the rumor mill got started. Fortunately, the company is in good shape and strong hands and I feel good about that.
>
> I am optimistic that my medical treatment will be successful, and that I will be involved with the company for a long time to come.

Bronson soldiered through the middle spring, coming to his office several days each week. He also attended most meetings of the Vanderbilt capital campaign committee, which he had previously agreed to chair.

His passing now set in motion an intensive period of planning by his family for the future of the family businesses. Together with a handful of trusted advisers, Martha and her adult children would sort out new roles for Bronson's heirs. In their elaborate estate planning, Bronson and Martha had already agreed on many things.

The first was that Bronson had discussed with Martha his wish that, upon his death, she would succeed him as the chairman of the board of Ingram Industries Inc. He also instructed Chip Lacy, whom Bronson had hired as part of the acquisition of Micro D, and who had risen to become president of Ingram Industries in 1993, to help his sons Orrin, John, and David continue their preparation for leadership roles in the various family businesses.

Lacy soon became caught up in a governance dispute with Martha, relating to the planning for Ingram Micro's future, in which Lacy wanted to play a more dominant role. As a result, he ended up leaving his position in the executive offices of Ingram Industries. However, he was given a seat on the corporation's board, and proved to be one of its most effective and respected members.

Orrin and John were then named co-presidents by the Ingram Industries board, which Martha now chaired. David, the youngest of the Ingram sons, who had run the video products distributor Ingram Entertainment, took his company independent in 1996. That same year, Ingram Micro filed for its initial public offering.

In sharing the co-president duties, Orrin and John continued their evolving executive roles on either side of the Ingram house. They had begun their informal apprenticeships as teenagers. Now, the senior Ingram executives with top-line responsibilities for the book and barge operations understood that their duties were, in part, to help Orrin and John prepare for leadership in the family businesses. All this had been part of Bronson's plan. At the Barge Company, where Orrin would eventually become chairman and CEO, his early mentor was Neil Diehl, the company president. John's early mentors in the book company were chiefly Phil Pfeffer, Lee Synnott, and Mike Lovett.

* * *

THE WORD "INTRAPRENEUR," FIRST COINED in a 1978 paper titled "Intra-Corporate Entrepreneurship," by Gifford Pinchot III and Elizabeth S. Pinchot, describes a business leader who drives the development of innovative products or services from inside an established company. An intrapreneur is able to find and embrace new ideas that the company may, with sufficient focus and capital, transform into the future of the company. During the 1980s, the term became a popular part of the business vocabulary. In 1985, *Newsweek* quoted Apple chairman Steve Jobs using it to describe the team that developed the Macintosh computer: "a group of people going, in essence, back to the garage, but in a large company."

Pfeffer, who likes using the term "intrapreneur" himself, played that creative role for Ingram during the middle years of acceleration. In 1995, when John inherited the book business upon his father's death, it was clear that the younger generation of company leaders had inherited a new and different world. As a result, they took the family business in new directions, bringing the spirit of intrapreneurship to new heights within Ingram.

The intrapreneurship driven by John and his team would eventually lead to a sustained period of continued growth and profitability for the family business. But first would come an era of uncertainty and turmoil. Technological change was continuing to accelerate, new forces and players were entering the field, and the structure of the book business was evolving rapidly.

The Ingram Book Company's response to these challenges would rely on a shrewd mix of business wits, adroit timing, constant experimentation, and aggressive technological adaptation, managed by a seasoned executive team carefully deploying the "patient capital" available to a large, successful, privately held business—and all orchestrated by a youthful intrapreneur driving the organization forward.

12
Lightning in a Bottle

W hat would become one of the most striking intrapreneurial triumphs of John Ingram's career started in 1996 with a conversation inside Ingram's book distribution center in La Vergne, Tennessee.

John and his friend YS Chi were walking through the super warehouse, surveying its vast arrays of tall metal shelving that rose, row upon row, thirty feet above the floor. It was a vista reminiscent of the closing scene of the film *Raiders of the Lost Ark*, in which a lone workman pushes a crate containing the hidden ark itself into a storage shelf, one of thousands of shelves that seem to recede into infinity. But in La Vergne, the tall racks were stacked with books. The enormous assortment of some 300,000 different book titles, each one available almost immediately to any Ingram customer, represented a core part of the company's value proposition. But each unsold book on those shelves also represented a cash investment by Ingram as well as a small but ever-mounting cost for warehousing and its associated expenses. And while some bestsellers and classic books were constantly being ordered, the demand for others—perhaps 200,000 of the 300,000 available titles—was weak and inconsistent.

John remembers turning to Chi, and asking, "Why in the world are we wallpapering the warehouse with all these books?"

At first, Chi wasn't exactly sure what John was referring to. But then John added, "After all, why couldn't we be storing the content digitally and then printing the books off once they're ordered?"

It was a simple question, but the answer would be complicated. It would require an aggressive planning and development effort that would lead to the creation of an entirely new business unit for the Ingram enterprise—one that would eventually come to play a major role in shaping the future of the family business and of the entire global book industry.

* * *

John's simple but visionary question hadn't come out of the blue. The mid-1990s were a time of startling growth for a Texas-based maker of personal computers known as Dell Computer. Dell's youthful founder, Michael Dell, had conceived a way of responding to customer orders for his products while keeping stand-by inventories as low as possible. Rather than pulling a computer off a warehouse shelf, Dell invited customers to visit the company's website and select the design specifications for a custom-built computer from a list of options. Not only did this business model reduce inventory costs, it also eliminated the problem of unsold merchandise while enabling consumers to buy a specially designed machine with only the features they wanted. For a time, Dell's ingenious system appeared poised to take over the computer business. Perhaps inspired partly by this innovation, John hoped to introduce a similar approach to the book business: "First sell the book, then produce the book."

Up to this point, the Ingram companies were not directly involved in the manufacturing of books. Publishers would acquire the rights to manuscripts from authors, put them through an editorial process, then have the book interiors and covers designed by artists, typographers, and graphic designers— all processes that, by the 1990s, were overwhelmingly performed using digital tools. The resulting electronic files would then be sent to outside printing companies, which would use them to print the books and bind them in paperback or cloth covers. (Generations earlier, book publishers had often owned and managed their own printing and binding facilities, but by the mid-twentieth century, these operations had virtually all been outsourced.)

Decisions surrounding the manufacturing of the first printing of a new book were complicated and important. Of course, it was (and is) important to introduce a new book at a propitious time for marketing, publicizing, and promoting it. Diet books are usually published in January to appeal to the many readers who make New Year's resolutions to lose weight; inspirational books for new college graduates arrive in bookstores in May or June; summer "beach reads" come out in July; and lavishly illustrated picture books appear in November so they can become holiday gifts a month later. This means that publishers have to work closely with printing firms to secure appropriate slots in their printing and binding schedules, especially when a hoped-for bestseller with a massive first printing is being planned.

The issue of quantity is even more fraught. The various steps in going from print-ready electronic files to finished books available to customers take several months to complete. They include printing and binding (two separate steps involving different machines in different sections of the manufacturing plant); packing and shipping; the receipt of books in the warehouse of a publisher, a wholesaler like Ingram, or a bookstore chain; a further shipment to an individual bookstore; and then, finally, the unpacking of books by bookstore employees and their placement on bookstore shelves—hopefully in the correct spots!

Because of this lengthy process—any step of which might be delayed by bad weather, technical breakdowns, work stoppages, financial woes, or other problems—the publisher must make a decision about how many copies of a book to produce several months before it will appear in stores. This means making an educated guess about likely future demand for the book. The evidence the publisher weighs in making this guess includes the identity of the author and his or her track record—it's safe to assume that a new book by a proven bestseller is likely to sell thousands of copies in the first few weeks, while a book by an unknown author will probably get off the ground slowly (if at all). The book's subject, its timeliness, the perceived quality of the writing, the enthusiasm displayed in advance reviews (if any), and the reactions of early readers within the publishing house (known as "buzz") are additional factors that will influence the print quantity decision. In addition, most publishers will also have a number of advance orders from individual bookstores and from bookstore chains to go on. Based on the cumulative impact of all these fragments of data, the publisher makes a decision whether to order the printing and binding of a small quantity of books (maybe as few as a thousand) or a large quantity (in the case of a likely bestseller, hundreds of thousands or even, in very rare cases, a few million).

This first-print decision is fraught with major implications for the publisher's bottom line. Print too many—for example, if the novel you considered a charming romance or a gripping thriller ends up leaving customers bored to tears—and you may have thousands of unsold copies to deal with. Some remain stuck in the publisher's own warehouse. Others get ordered by bookstores, only to go unsold, which means they end up being returned for full credit to the publishers. The storage or disposal of these unsold volumes comes at a significant cost. Thus, if the first-print order proves to have been too optimistic, the needless production costs as well as all the ancillary expenses eat heavily into the publisher's profit margin.

On the other hand, if you print too few copies of a book, you may find yourself facing a situation in which customers are clamoring for a book that has turned out to be far more popular than expected—but with no inventory available. Depending on seasonal fluctuations in demand and other factors (including the size and clout of the publisher), it may take anywhere from two to five weeks to get a reprint order into the printing company's schedule—by which time the demand for the book may have completely died out. This frustrating situation is less common than the problem of overprinting—but it can be just as costly to the publisher, and more upsetting to the author, who will go to the grave convinced that a potential megahit was strangled in the cradle by a publisher's overly cautious printing decision.

Now throw in one additional pressure—the fact that the unit cost for printing and binding a book goes down dramatically the larger the number of copies produced at one time. This means a publisher may be sorely tempted to increase a print run from, say, eight thousand copies to ten thousand copies in order to take advantage of a "price break" that goes into effect when the larger quantity is reached—despite the fact that ten thousand copies may be more than the particular book requires.

Against this complicated economic background, you can see why John's idea of printing books only after orders had been received was potentially revolutionary. Print-on-demand, or POD (as this new technology came to be called), could eliminate most of the guesswork involved in predicting future demand for a book by tying print quantities directly to demonstrated demand in the form of orders actually placed. If it could actually be done, it would dramatically reduce the uncertainty and financial risk faced by publishers, as well as improve the cash flow positions of book retailers. And for Ingram itself, it would represent a natural expansion and enhancement of the company's core value proposition—its vast, almost unlimited array of book titles available—without demanding a huge increase in investment capital.

But there was the rub: Could it actually be done?

As the members of the Ingram team examined what it would take to realize John's vision, the complexity of the challenge quickly became obvious. POD would require a high level of technical and systems skills and ingenuity. New software programs of great complexity would need to be designed.

An even greater challenge would be integrating the twin processes of printing and binding. Not only were these separate jobs, performed by different machines, but their operating speeds were very different. Modern offset printing machines, the dominant technology in book publishing, can produce the large sheets that are folded and cut to make "signatures" of sixteen or thirty-two book pages very quickly. But binding the pages is much slower. The difference in speed means that integrating the two processes is very challenging—and doing so automatically is particularly difficult.

There were other technical barriers to realizing John's POD dream. Offset printing is extremely fast once a print run of a single book title is underway, but the preparation process, called make-ready, is labor-intensive and time-consuming. It involves clamping thin metal plates bearing the images of the pages onto printing cylinders, adjusting ink settings, and running one or more test runs to make sure the sheets are being printed correctly. The inefficiency of make-ready is one reason that offset printing would be an extremely wasteful and expensive process to use in producing one or a few copies of a book. Part of the projected benefit of POD would be the ability to produce just as many copies as needed, and to do so affordably—provided the entire make-ready process could be eliminated or drastically reduced

This, then, was the challenge that Ingram took on.

Probably unsurprisingly, Ingram wasn't the only company thinking about how to take advantage of the latest digital technologies to bring new efficiencies to the production of books. Publisher Jason Epstein had been pondering the same possibility. Epstein had long been considered one of the most creative thinkers in publishing. While working at Doubleday in the mid-1950s, Epstein had created the Anchor Books imprint to publish "quality paperbacks" for sale in bookstores rather than the traditional newsstand outlets; within a few years, the so-called trade paperback revolution would be in full swing, with similar imprints at virtually every publisher. In 1979, Epstein helped cofound the Library of America, a publisher dedicated to producing fine editions of classic American literature, and, in 1986, he launched the Reader's Catalog, which used the then-leading-edge technology of toll-free telephone ordering to make a huge array of backlist books easily available.

With this track record of innovations behind him, when Epstein talked, people in the world of books listened.

In 1999, he gave a series of lectures at the New York Public Library describing the possibilities for what he called an "ATM for books"—a low-priced, automatic printing and binding machine that could be installed in a bookstore, library, newsstand, or other retailer. This device would print a book from a digital file on demand, making almost any title available almost anywhere.

Epstein soon discovered that a St. Louis inventor named Jeff Marsh had already built a prototype for such a machine. In 2003, with help from Marsh, Epstein cofounded a company called On Demand Books to commercialize the device, which they called the Espresso Book Machine. In some ways, it worked brilliantly. It could produce an individual book, including printing and binding, within three to five minutes. Which sounds fantastic—except that, in a retail setting, this is actually not a very satisfactory performance. What if you want to order a specific book while visiting a busy downtown bookstore—and you discover that you are tenth in line behind other patrons? Suddenly the wait for your book has mushroomed to almost an hour, which is not what most people think of as "instant." For this reason, among others, Espresso Book

Machine never really took off; to this day, the number of units actually in operation in bookstores, libraries, and other venues has never exceeded a few dozen.

John Ingram, of course, had a different business model in mind. Rather than serving individual readers by printing books for them in locations around the world, his idea was to drastically improve the efficiency of the book supply chain much closer to its source. Readers wouldn't get their books "instantly." But the supply chain improvements made possible through POD, in combination with the new efficiencies that the Internet would produce, would end up vastly expanding the universe of books available to readers—perhaps an even more impressive benefit.

* * *

THE NEW BUSINESS WOULD BE called Lightning Print Inc., and John delegated the task of building it to Chi. Their first hire was Larry Brewster.

Brewster was not a veteran of the book industry but a specialist in modern computer-guided printing systems. Tall and lanky, Brewster had been a college basketball star at the University of Florida. He was selected by the San Antonio Spurs in the 1978 NBA draft. He joined IBM instead, and for the next fourteen years worked in its printing systems division, which brought him to Nashville. When Chi contacted him in 1997, Brewster also had established his own private consulting business in computer systems.

"Ingram was one of our customers at IBM, and I had met with them before," Brewster remembers. "They were looking for somebody to come in and work out the business case for on-demand printing and get it started. I went and interviewed with John Ingram and Lee Synnott, and they hired me in April 1997. We figured out pretty early that we wanted a technology partner to figure out how to do this. It would require technology and resource experience that was not then at Ingram. We got involved with IBM and Xerox and put together a bid. They became very interested because they knew Ingram and the role Ingram played in the book industry's value chain." At this time, Xerox was a leader in printing systems technology. IBM offered industrial laser printers used for report production but was not involved in the book business, though Brewster was aware some IBM executives had imagined a promising growth opportunity in digital book printing.

Soon the Ingram executive team put together a strategy to outsource the early work of developing Lightning Print. The result was a new joint venture among Ingram, IBM, and Danka Business Systems. This is how Danka's Edward J. Marino joined the Ingram team. In 1999, Marino would become

Lightning Print's first president, with Brewster as his general manager and second-in-command.

"We needed Lightning Print to be separate and independent from the rest of Ingram," Brewster remembers.

> It required an entrepreneurial spirit and a technology knowledge and a willingness to move fast—things that were really not at Ingram at that point. It was a great place to work, but not like a technology-oriented company.
>
> One of the best things John Ingram did was that he put Lightning off to the side. He made us a different company. That was key to the whole thing working. If we'd gotten bogged down with the rest of Ingram, it would not be the right place for a company like Lightning. We would have been "the thing on the side." John and YS were very smart to pull it out and make it separate—to give us our own structure and funding and make it independent.
>
> We could've turned a profit sooner, but it wouldn't have been the best thing for the business. You can do things to restrict growth and improve profitability. Part of that seven-year period, we decided to get in the ebook business. If you look at it alone, it was a loss and didn't make money, but on the other side it brought in the technology to handle huge amounts of data that contributed to the success of the print-on-demand business. People thought POD wasn't going to work long-term. But we kept plowing along.

In line with that initial "Why wallpaper the warehouse?" question that John had raised with Chi that day when they walked among the high shelves in La Vergne, the new business concept now took tangible shape. Brewster, among others, remembers:

> Our whole concept was "one book at a time"—where all the books would be stored on the computer, and you'd print out books that were needed by publishers or booksellers on that day. This required a tremendous amount of software innovation that could operate at the speed the orders came in. The idea was a little ahead of the technology—not only the printing technology but the ability to store these books digitally and bring them online very fast. That's what was different and new. Nobody else had tried to do this.

"I loved the business model," Marino says.

John Ingram's vision back then was to really make this not some small supply-chain strategy to support the book company, but he saw the value of the digital technology in creating new and better business models in the book business. What he leaned on us for was the combination of good vision and good execution. Others had come at this from the standpoint of print. We did not. We looked at it as an information technology business, not as a book printing business. What that allowed us to do was treat every order as a unique product and do it in a very efficient fashion. It was all data to us. That was one of the breakthroughs.

Lightning Print produced its first book for a customer in January 1998—a mystery titled *The Hanged Man*, by Trish MacGregor. Lightning printed one thousand copies of the bound galleys of the MacGregor book for Kensington Publishing, a New York–based publisher, to be distributed to the media and booksellers as part of the pre-publication publicity for the book.

Just producing a product using the new POD technology was an impressive feat. But for publishers, who licensed ownership of the content of books from authors, it was not only a matter of data and technical competence but also trust. Marino recalls:

> The other part that was really important was getting publishers to participate—the owners of the book content. I remember, very early on, YS and I were talking to Larry Kirshbaum, the longtime head of the Time Warner Book Group, in New York.
>
> Kirshbaum said, "So, I'm going to give you my precious content, and you're going to store it in your data system. And at the end of the month I get a statement on what you've sold and then I get a check?"
>
> I responded, "Exactly! That's what we'll do!"
>
> The only reason that worked is because Ingram was a trusted partner to these publishers. That trust had been hard-won by Ingram over a long period of time.

Lightning's acquisition of publisher content became a long march. At the end of 1998, after a year in business, Lightning Print had about 1,500 titles in its library. A year later, the number had grown to 5,380 titles. Not bad—but not yet enough. The internal business plan had set a benchmark of having 100,000 titles in its digital database as the crossover point to profitability for Lightning Print.

Ultimately, transforming Lightning from a fascinating novelty into a profitable business would require great patience, both in the boardroom at Ingram Industries as well as among even the most senior management team at La Vergne.

When it all began, in the mid-1990s, the notion of "print on demand" as a new core function of Ingram's business was seriously questioned inside the company. John remembers this early phase of Lightning's development as the time when some insiders dismissed POD as "John's little problem."

"I would go to those board meetings, and people would get a little testy," Marino recalls. "The issue was money. The business consumed a lot of cash. We weren't profitable yet. We needed to hit a hundred thousand books to become profitable."

Unwavering support from a handful of key individuals made all the difference during these challenging early years. Marino and Brewster recalled one Ingram Industries corporate board meeting where the discussion about Lightning Print's prospects went on for many minutes. Then, from the head of the table, chairman Martha Ingram spoke up. "Every now and then," she reminded the directors, "you have to plant some new trees in the forest."

"That ended the discussion," Marino says.

Much as Ingram had done during the infancy of its microfiche reader, the company used its booth at the 1998 BookExpo to showcase the new technology. The Ingram display became a center of attention at that year's convention. The massive setup featured a real print line, with a roll of paper on one end feeding into an IBM 4100 digital book printer and producing an actual bound paperback book coming off the end of the line.

"People were amazed at it," Brewster remembers. "I had people tell me it was the biggest thing they'd ever seen at a BookExpo. Between speaking and demos, I remember being totally exhausted after that convention. But it really opened people's eyes that this wasn't just an idea. Publishers started thinking seriously about print on demand."

There were also some early wins that bolstered the buzz around Ingram's new capability.

One occurred in 1998, when the University of Virginia Press published *Thomas Jefferson and Sally Hemings: An American Controversy,* by Annette Gordon-Reed. The director of the press phoned Brewster with good news: he had been alerted that that title was to be named an Oprah's Book Club selection within a few days, likely to create enormous new demand. But there was no time to rev up an offset print order. Lightning delivered two thousand copies, which got UVP through the early tight spot until the new print run produced through conventional offset printing could be brought online.

Many of the other early publishers who signed on with Lightning were university-based academic presses. These were a natural fit for Lightning Print because they publish so many long-lived books in short print runs.

One of the first was Cambridge University Press in the United Kingdom, and its managing director Michael Holdsworth became a spirited advocate for the new on-demand mode. Among commercial publishers, John Wiley & Sons, a venerable independent house with important publishing programs in the academic, professional, and trade book arenas, was one of the first to embrace POD. George Stanley was vice president of sales there at this point, and he remembers both the initial doubts expressed by Wiley executives and their gradual embrace of the technology's potential.

"They took it slowly," Stanley says. "They were questioning how far this could go, how much content information did they have to give up, where that information was going, those types of things. But Wiley was willing to give it a shot. We stuck our toe in, and over time it slowly got bigger and bigger."

The early promise showed by Lightning Print was impressive. But the late 1990s was a time when hundreds of innovative business ideas built on digital technologies were rearing their heads. Some, like Amazon, eBay, and Google, would go on to become massive long-term successes. Others would flame out, especially in 2001 when the so-called dot-com boom gave way to the dot-com bust. As the decade came to an end, it wasn't yet clear whether Lightning Print would be one of the survivors.

13

Digitization Rocks the Industry

By the start of the new millennium, Ingram's Lightning Print was showing how the process of manufacturing printed books could be transformed through digital technologies. At the same time, digital transformation was just beginning to impact the book business from other, different directions. One of these assaults on the traditional book industry was being launched by an innovative businessman named Jeff Bezos.

It might seem laughable now, with a quarter-century of hindsight, but Jeff Bezos and his company Amazon were not taken seriously by many in the traditional book industry when they first came into view. In fact, very few understood what Amazon wanted to be.

One who did was Art Carson, at Ingram.

Carson first met Bezos in 1993 at a meeting of the Pacific Northwest Booksellers Association in Roseburg, Oregon. At the time, Bezos was researching the best location for a headquarters for his contemplated online bookselling operation. Seattle was one of the cities on his short list.

At this same meeting, Ingram would announce its plans to build a new Roseburg distribution center. When it opened the next year, this new facility would be capable of providing next-day delivery service to booksellers across the Seattle and Pacific Northwest regions. This intrigued Bezos. As we've seen, Ingram had by this time improved its own distribution and delivery systems to the point that it could provide next-day delivery for most books to most bookstores that were close to an Ingram warehouse. Bezos realized that an operation located in Seattle (only about 350 miles from Roseburg) would be able to get next-day access to Ingram's vast inventory of books from all publishers.

Carson arranged to visit Bezos at his then-tiny headquarters. "I remember calling on him and his two key employees," Carson recalls. "Shel Kaplan was a programmer, and Nicholas Lovejoy was in human resources. Jeff told them that I was the first book industry person to call on him. I recall he had two computer servers with name tags on them: They called them 'Bert' and 'Ernie.'"

(Years later, Jeff Bezos was a keynote speaker at the national American Booksellers Association convention. When he spotted Art Carson across the room, he pointed toward him and yelled, "There's the first guy I ever met from the book business!")

Back in 1993, Bezos did end up choosing Seattle as the headquarters for his new company. The proximity to Ingram's Roseburg distribution center was one reason. Availability of next-day delivery from Roseburg greatly enhanced one of Amazon's most powerful innovations: the "promise date" that told customers exactly when they could expect to receive the book or books they'd purchased. Depending on the location of the ultimate customer, next-day delivery from Ingram to Amazon meant Amazon could generally offer a promise date within three or four days, or at most a week. Back in the mid-1990s, that was an impressive feat—one that converted countless people who'd previously been reluctant to switch from brick-and-mortar stores to online shopping.

Thus, in Amazon's early days, before the company had built its own extensive chain of warehouses (stockpiling vast amounts of inventory not just of books but of many other forms of merchandise), Ingram's ultra-efficient logistics provided the almost-frictionless system Bezos needed to make his new company the online retailer of choice.

On the other hand, there was one aspect of Ingram's inventory management system that Amazon deliberately chose not to use—ironically, because it was, in a sense, too efficient. This was the Ingram database of book inventory, the updated descendent of the microfiche system from 1973 that had originally vaulted Ingram into its powerful role in the world of book wholesaling.

By the mid-1990s, there was one other book database in the industry that was comparable in its scope to Ingram's. That was the database maintained by Baker & Taylor, which was still the world's leading wholesaler serving the library market. Bezos and his team studied both the Ingram and the B&T databases, and they discovered a curious difference between the two. The Ingram database was frequently "scrubbed" of titles that were out of print or otherwise unavailable from publishers. By contrast, the B&T database was rarely updated in this way, which meant that a growing number of titles would remain on the B&T list despite the fact that requests to buy them would be fruitless.

Bezos considered how this difference between the two databases would impact customers searching for book titles online. Suppose you visited the Amazon website looking for a book with a particular title and author name— a book that, as it happened, had gone out of print. If Amazon tapped the Ingram database, the search would yield no results, since the database would have had the out-of-print title removed at some point. By contrast, if Amazon made the same request using the B&T database, the search would recognize the title and produce a message saying, in effect, "This title is no longer available."

Bezos realized that the latter outcome would be much better for Amazon. After all, if a customer visiting Amazon found that a certain title search simply produced no result, he or she would most likely conclude, "Oh, well, Amazon just doesn't carry that book. I guess I should search elsewhere." And eventually, the customer might even find the book—for example, on a website maintained by a seller of used books. (This was before the day when Amazon began selling used books through a network of independent booksellers around the country.) In any case, the customer would have been lost by Amazon.

By contrast, if the same customer received a message from Amazon saying, "This title is no longer available," the reaction would likely be quite different. Most often, the customer would conclude—accurately—that the book had gone out of print, and would probably move on to shopping for some other title, without leaving the Amazon site.

Thus, the B&T database, though in some ways less accurate and complete than Ingram's, provided more useful information for Amazon and its customers. Which is why Amazon made the B&T database its source document of choice when tracking down books—even though it usually made the actual book purchases through Ingram instead.

There's one other odd twist in the story of the early years of the Amazon-Ingram connection. Steven Mason, who served as president and CEO of Ingram Book Company from 1983 to 1989, and later helped greatly expand Ingram's international book business, recalls noticing as early as the mid-1990s the popularity of online shopping in Germany—including shopping for books.

"I thought that Ingram could be using the Internet to sell books direct to consumers in the United States," Mason recalls. He actually wrote a letter proposing such a plan, but Bronson Ingram and others in the company were reluctant to launch a business that would compete with its best customers—the retail booksellers. They turned down the idea.

Convinced it could work, Mason asked whether there'd be any objection to members of his family running with the concept. When this was okayed, Mason's two sons leased a storefront office about three quarters of a mile from Ingram's warehouse in La Vergne. In partnership with a couple of young German friends, they launched an online bookseller known as Bookserve. The business enjoyed some success; in these early days, Bookserve could compete with Amazon and even became, for a time, one of Ingram's top ten accounts. And in September 1996, a *New York Times* article described what happened when a customer ordered an obscure travel guide from Amazon's already sizeable online catalog:

An order is made electronically with a credit card number. A company E-mail note confirms a shipping charge of $7.95 for the $10.95 paperback. Later Amazon issues more E-mail, explaining delivery will take four to six weeks, followed by another note stating the book is not available.

However, the book, which was also ordered from David and Michael Mason, who run an Internet bookstore, Bookserve, from a Nashville area strip mall, does appear on a porch step three days later—and at half Amazon's shipping fee. "Our main focus is finding books," Michael said. "Their focus is P.R. and marketing."

At least in this one instance, little Bookserve had beaten Amazon at its own game—stellar customer service. To be fair, the article went on to quote Bezos as saying that Amazon had been mistakenly informed by the book's publisher that the title was out of print.

Still, it's fascinating to imagine how different history might have been if Steven Mason's kids had gone on to outcompete Bezos. In reality, Bookserve was sold to a competitor a few years later and has long since vanished from the scene. And Amazon went on to claim a leading role in the online bookselling world—ironically, in part because Bezos had never intended to remain simply a bookseller. Amazon was willing to sell books at steeply discounted prices, forgoing potential profits, because its long-term goal was to use bookselling as a stepping stone on its way to building "the everything store." The company might not make any money on selling a particular book to a particular customer— but in the long run, it would profit handsomely from the many other products it would later sell to that same customer.

When your entire business is built on books, you can't afford to treat books as a mere "loss leader." Because Amazon was not so much a bookseller as a highly sophisticated customer acquisition system, Bezos could and did.

* * *

By the mid-1990s, Carson and Mason may have recognized the enormous potential of the business that Bezos was building. But many others did not. Carson recalls tracking Amazon's weekly purchases from Ingram with Mason and marveling at the steady volume growth they showed. One day, John Ingram got a glimpse of one of those printouts. "Those numbers are pretty amazing," he commented.

"Well, that's what Amazon is doing with the World Wide Web," Carson replied.

"What the hell is the World Wide Web?" John asked.

Very soon, John and much of the rest of the world would be learning the answer to that question.

Ed Morrow is a Vermont bookstore owner who was then president of the American Booksellers Association. Morrow recalls talking with many of his members about the new competitive effect that Amazon had introduced to their market.

"I remember when I was first trying to explain Amazon to my fellow booksellers, who thought that Jeff Bezos was the devil incarnate, and he may well be, but we're seeing him on a different level and scale now than anyone thought about then," Morrow said. "My argument was, 'Look, this guy is a genius. He's created something here that's going to go beyond this, and we have to deal with it. It's not going to go away.' And they didn't believe that. Soon he started to lose money due to his discounting of book prices, and when he was burning money, everybody thought, 'Oh, he's gonna crash.'"

But Bezos was not about to crash, and the independent booksellers would be among those impacted by his rise.

This wasn't the first big challenge that the independents had faced. Market forces, including consolidation across the industry, were already working against their interests. B&N's superstores had offered consumers new experiences and wider product choice and exerted new competitive pressures on smaller bookstores. This became quickly visible—and increasingly controversial in the book trade—as independent stores across the United States began to shut their doors. The ABA saw its membership decline by half over the decade of the 1990s. Total ABA members dropped from 5,200 bookstores in 1991 to 3,300 in 1998.

But now Amazon began to mount a new threat to independent booksellers. Over time, with its deeply discounted prices for trade books, Amazon began to draw retail business away from the traditional "brick-and-mortar" bookstores. By 2002, the number of independent booksellers in ABA would decline even further, to 2,191.

During this turbulent decade of change in book retailing, Ingram, which supplied all types of bookstores, as well as Amazon, steadfastly remained focused on its own neutrality. Senior Ingram executives in Nashville and La Vergne liked to remind their associates that it was never their company's place to take sides. "We served all bookstores, from tiny independents to the biggest chains," Lovett said, "and, for a time, Ingram played a large part in leveling the retail playing field."

* * *

Meanwhile, as Amazon was building what would become the principal power in the world of online bookselling, another digital disruption to publishing was taking shape. A number of pioneers were experimenting with the concept of replacing printed books altogether, abandoning the centuries-old technology invented by Gutenberg in favor of electronic books to be read on the screen of a computer, tablet, or other device.

Electronic books first emerged in the mid-1990s. But for more than a decade, they gained little traction in the publishing world. A range of companies tried to popularize the ebook concept, leaving a host of varied failures in their wake.

Some of the earliest ebook experiments used desktop computer screens to deliver book content. The interfaces were clunky, and a bulky monitor was far less convenient and flexible to use than a traditional book, which could be easily tucked into a purse or briefcase. But when computer makers began finding ways to make their devices smaller and portable, the idea of the ebook got a new life. During the 1990s and the early 2000s, personal digital assistants (PDAs) from companies like Psion, IBM, Apple, and Palm featured screens on which texts could be displayed—including book texts. However, book content for PDAs was generally delivered using the portable document format (PDF) invented by Adobe. This meant it wasn't readily adaptable for different-sized screens, which fragmented the ebook market and therefore sharply limited its economic value to publishers. And the screens themselves didn't provide an enjoyable reading experience: they were small, low-resolution, glare-prone, and fatiguing to the eyes. Most readers who tested the earliest ebooks agreed that their disadvantages outweighed their benefits.

Still, tech companies and publishers continued to experiment with ebooks. In 2000, the popular author Stephen King caused a stir when he published a novella titled *Riding the Bullet* exclusively as a digital text for download from the Internet. During the first forty-eight hours of its availability, the book was downloaded by over 500,000 King fans, most of whom read the text on PalmPilot PDAs—unless the encryption caused their devices to crash, as many apparently did. Industry observers took note of the hubbub, but most were only moderately impressed. It wasn't clear how readers would be able to learn about and purchase ebooks by authors without brand-name bestseller credentials. One journalist commented, "The media worked hard to turn King's insurgent act into a writers' revolution. It is probably not. Most writers, unlike King, can't book themselves on the 'Today' show and 'Good Morning America' on the day of their launch." What was missing was a viable ebook platform that would be embraced by hundreds of thousands of readers as a steady source of great reading content.

In 2003, Sony introduced the Sony Reader, a handheld device that could be loaded with content through the consumer's computer. This device seemed to promise a market breakthrough because it employed a new, vastly improved type of display screen known as E Ink. But the original Sony Reader, launched in Japan as the LIBRIé, never got off the ground because of a fatal flaw in the company's business model.

The story was explained in an interview with Sony's Yoshitaka Ukita by authors Adrian Slywotzky and Karl Weber in their 2011 book *Demand*. As Ukita recalls, the LIBRIé was a technological marvel. Not only was the screen remarkably paperlike in its appearance—crisp black characters contrasting sharply with a pale gray background—but it was glare-proof and easy to read in practically all lighting conditions. The machine was almost exactly the size and weight of a typical paperback book, promising a familiar, comfortable experience for avid readers. And, of course, it would be backed by Sony, one of the world's great technology brands.

But when Ukita met with ten of Japan's leading book publishers in 2003 to introduce the LIBRIé, they proceeded to sabotage the product in classic passive-aggressive style. While expressing their admiration for the new device and promising to support it fully, they agreed only to provide digital rights to one hundred book titles each. And although one thousand titles may sound at first like an impressive number, it's the equivalent of just one small corner of the typical bookstore—not enough to retain the interest of most booklovers. What's more, the ebooks would be available only for a sixty-day paid rental. If you got distracted and failed to finish a book in that time—or wanted to reread it later—you'd find it vanished from your LIBRIé.

In short, the LIBRIé was doomed to be a frustrating experience for avid readers—who of course would be the most important market for any electronic reading device. Sales languished.

Sony didn't give up on the E Ink technology. In 2006, it released a new device called the Sony Reader, which had access to a larger collection of twenty thousand titles. But even this assortment proved to be too skimpy to make major inroads into the habits of booklovers.

The breakthrough finally came in November 2007, when Amazon introduced the Kindle. Like the Sony Reader, the Kindle used E Ink to produce an attractive, booklike screen image. But Bezos and his team shrewdly avoided Sony's business model mistake. They laid the foundation for their device by investing months in courting and winning commitments from the major US publishers—all of whom had already come to know, respect, and even fear Amazon as one of the major distributors of their books. On the day Amazon launched the Kindle, it proudly announced that 88,000 titles were available—the equivalent of a well-stocked independent bookstore—including practically every title then featured on the *New York Times* bestseller lists. Devoted book readers had finally been given an electronic reading experience that was worth their while.

By the end of 2008, some half a million Kindle devices had been sold. During 2009, two new Kindle models with varying features and price points were released, the first entries in a growing lineup of versions that continues to expand to this day. Amazon had almost single-handedly created a robust ebook market and seized a leading position that it still retains.

The success of the Kindle line of devices was followed by other ebook readers, including the Nook from Barnes & Noble and the Kobo from an upstart Canadian company. Other varieties of handheld electronic devices began incorporating book reading into their array of supported features. Apple had already begun transforming the world of electronic phones with its iPhone, the first so-called smartphone, which debuted in 2007. The company followed this up in April 2010 with the iPad, the first so-called tablet. Simultaneously, Apple launched its own online ebook store, selling content that could be read on either smartphones or tablets.

In November 2010, assessing the rise of ebooks, the *Times* reporter Julie Bosman, who covered the book industry, described "an acknowledgment of the growing sales and influence of digital publishing." The editors announced that, starting in 2011, they would begin publishing ebook bestseller lists alongside their traditional lists of hardcover and paperback bestsellers. In explaining the change, Bosman cited sales data:

> E-book sales have risen steeply in 2010, spurred by the growing popularity of the Amazon Kindle and by the release of the Apple iPad in April. According to the Association of American Publishers, which receives sales data from publishers, e-book sales in the first nine months of 2010 were $304.6 million, up from $105.6 million from the same period in 2009, a nearly 190 percent increase.

The ebook explosion threw many in the book business into a tizzy. Some were terrified by the prospect that ebooks might decimate publishing much the way music downloads had decimated the record companies following the introduction of Apple's iPod in 2001. And many were especially worried about the growing power of Amazon, which had already been selling printed books at a steep discount from the publisher's list price. Amazon was willing to accept minuscule profit margins or even an actual loss on some sales in return for a big and growing share of the online market. What if they applied the same philosophy to ebooks? Given the fact that ebooks involved manufacturing and shipping costs of essentially nothing, why couldn't Amazon price them ultra-aggressively—say, at ninety-nine cents apiece—and perhaps destroy the market for traditional books altogether?

The leaders of Ingram were also concerned over this new development. Over its first twenty-five years, Ingram's very infrastructure had been grounded in the physical transportation of books and related products, developing ever more efficient conveyance of those products from publisher's presses to booksellers and library shelves. Outstanding service and large product selection had been Ingram's calling card, its brand expertise in adding value for storefronts as well as online retailers with the best of speed, selection, and service.

But how far would this digital trend go? Would physical books become an artifact of an older age? Would booksellers and librarians need to change their skills for this new age, acquiring and distributing content in a dramatically new way? And if so, what would happen to Ingram? A new future dominated by digital books, transmitted not by trucks but over the Internet, would seem to hold little promise for the wholesaler of printed pages.

For a time, it appeared as though Amazon would indeed use its market position to make ebooks ultra-affordable, regardless of the impact on print book sales. The early Kindle devices themselves were expensive—priced as high as $399—largely because both the technology required to include dial-up connectivity and the dial-up service itself, paid for by Amazon, were costly. (Today's familiar Wi-Fi service was just beginning to become popular in 2007.) To compensate, Amazon pushed ebook prices as low as possible. What better way for Amazon to juice Kindle sales than by making thousands of ebook titles available for just a buck or two apiece? As a result, early Kindle adopters tended to be voracious readers who were willing to spend big bucks for a device that promised to make tons of books available in a cheap, convenient format.

For several years, sales of ebooks rose rapidly. John describes this phenomenon as largely a matter of "pipeline filling." As readers purchased the new Kindles, iPads, and other devices, or received them as holiday gifts, they also bought collections of ebooks to download. By 2013, ebook unit sales had risen to represent about 25 percent of all book sales. Some observers extrapolated from this upward curve to a world in which printed books were a specialty item of interest to just a minority.

The traditional publishers found this prospect alarming. Five of the so-called Big Six publishers responded by joining forces with Apple. They agreed on a new way of selling ebooks called "agency pricing," which allowed the publishers to set prices that the retailer could not reduce through discounting. Under agency pricing, the fixed consumer price—$14.99, for example—would be split between the retailer (Apple) and the publisher on a 30/70 percent basis.

An uproar ensued, leading to a complicated legal tangle. The Justice Department sued Apple and the five publishers for price fixing, and won the suit. Agency pricing was prohibited, and sanctions were imposed on the publishers. But after a few years, the sanctions expired—and today, both Apple and Amazon apply the agency pricing model to sales of ebooks. As a result, the biggest commercial publishers now maintain relatively high ebook prices—often higher than the prices that Amazon chooses to charge for printed editions of the same books. (Many smaller publishers and indie authors, however, price their ebooks low.)

Partially as a result of this pricing anomaly, ebooks have not gone on to wipe out the market for traditional printed books. Once the novelty of the new electronic readers wore off, sales of the devices leveled off—and so did sales of ebooks, as most readers had completed the pipeline-filling process. Ebook sales then hit a plateau. They have remained at about the same relative level ever since, representing about a quarter of book sales units (and a bit less than this as a percentage of publisher revenues).

Apparently, many booklovers like to read on electronic screens—but many more prefer the traditional look, feel, and smell of a printed book. Players in the industry, from publishers to retailers, have found ways to satisfy both. And the economics of the book business, while never extremely lucrative, have not been decimated by a flood of almost-free digital products.

* * *

WHILE THE TWISTS AND TURNS of the ebook saga were unfolding, Ingram was continuing to pursue its mission of transforming the process of manufacturing traditional printed books through its digital print-on-demand operation, Lightning Source. (The name was changed from Lightning Print in mid-2000, in part due to the growing realization that book publishing was evolving to include a range of non-print products, including ebooks.)

Once the technological challenges of POD had been met, the biggest business challenge was convincing book publishers to make their content available to Ingram in digital form. The in-flow of titles, each requiring decisions by the respective publisher, happened slowly at first. Then it happened fast. Eventually hundreds, then thousands, of book publishers began to find the new Lightning Source model appealing. Many were especially drawn to the possibility of being freed from the cost of warehousing thousands of unsold books. Publisher Jack Romanos recalls his own experience at Simon & Schuster: "We had 17,000 active backlist titles, and unfortunately had warehouses full of them. And continuing to make them available on a print-on-demand basis was appealing . . . Publishers were beginning to appreciate the value of that kind of printing."

Even as publishers started to discover the benefits of Lightning Source, it would take seven full years for the division to turn a profit for Ingram.

Complicating matters further was a lawsuit launched in 2001 by On Demand Machine Corporation (ODMC), a St. Louis-based business founded by inventor Harvey Ross. The suit claimed that the POD technologies used by both Lightning Source and Amazon infringed on a patent Ross had filed for his own single-copy printing device. In truth, Ross's machine was not a close match for Lightning Source's technology; it was a retail point-of-sale device more akin to Jason Epstein's Espresso Book Machine (developed by another St. Louis-based inventor, Jeff Marsh) than to Ingram's industrial POD system. But the lawsuit still gained some traction. Ross himself died in 2002, but ODMC pursued the case, and in 2004 it even won a $15 million jury verdict against Lightning Source.

Ingram immediately filed an appeal, but there was no guarantee it would be successful, which cast a pall over the future of Lightning Source. The willingness of Ingram Industries to support the business through these early travails is a testament to the company's persistent management style, as well as another example of the strategic benefits generated by Ingram's "patient capital" approach.

In 2004, thanks to the continuing growth of its digital book content inventory, Lightning Source's red ink turned black. Then, in 2006, the US Court of Appeals for the Federal Circuit overturned the verdict in the ODMC case, finding unanimously that "no reasonable jury could find infringement on the correct claim construction." With the burden of uncertainty created by the lawsuit lifted, Lightning Source was free to pursue growth unencumbered. The expanding enterprise became one of the best modern illustrations in American business of the benefits of a potent mixture: pairing a pioneering new idea with technical creativity and inventive team building, all under the guidance of an intrapreneurial leader.

In 2004, Lightning's industry-changing potential had become more widely recognized when Chris Anderson, the editor of *Wired* magazine, wrote an influential article titled "The Long Tail." Anderson's article, later the basis of a bestselling book, described changes he saw coming in the culture, particularly in traditional retail economics.

In Anderson's view, new technologies were introducing the possibilities for an important transition in the cultural marketplace from a focus on a few blockbuster hits to a broader lens that included lesser products whose aggregate value could be as great as, or even greater than, the value of the blockbusters. These "nonhits" constituted the "long tail" of the bell curve that graphically depicts the typical pattern of product sales. Anderson showed how the Internet and related tools were making it economically feasible to build profitable businesses based on selling long-tail products in industries from movies and music to video games—and, in particular, books. Anderson observed:

> What's really amazing about the Long Tail is the sheer size of it. Combine enough nonhits on the Long Tail and you've got a market bigger than the hits. Take books: The average Barnes & Noble carries 130,000 titles. Yet more than half of Amazon's book sales come from outside its top 130,000 titles. Consider the implication: If the Amazon statistics are any guide, the market for books that are not even sold in the average bookstore is larger than the market for those that are.

Obviously, this view had important implications for retailers of cultural products. Traditional retail economics dictate that stores focus on stocking the likely hits, because shelf space is both limited and expensive. The concept of the long tail suggests that retailers need to pay attention to nonhits as well. In the book world, superstores like those run by Barnes & Noble are well equipped to serve the many customers who are interested in out-of-the-mainstream topics, genres, and authors. But even better-equipped are online retailers like Amazon, which can take advantage of the Internet's virtually limitless data capacity by offering a catalog of products whose number is, for all practical purposes, infinite. A proliferating array of digital tools offers help in making the long tail of endless product choice even more readily accessible. These tools include powerful search engines like Google, the use of so-called metadata to make book listings and book contents themselves instantly searchable, online review sites that allow millions of ordinary people to promote their favorite products, recommendation engines that generate product suggestions customized to individual tastes, and much more.

Lightning Source was beautifully designed to help publishers take advantage of the long-tail phenomenon. Those thousands of backlist titles mentioned by

Romanos are mainly denizens of the long tail—niche products with small but persistent audiences that might sell one, two, five, or ten copies a year. Taken individually, these sales figures are too small to make it economical to do conventional print runs of five hundred or one thousand copies of such titles and then to warehouse them for the many years it might take to sell them all. But POD makes it possible to affordably produce one or a few copies as they are needed. Suddenly, it is feasible for a publisher to realize the aggregate sales potential of those thousands of "little" books.

A closely related benefit of the POD model for publishers is that no book need ever go out of print, the designation traditionally applied to published books that are no longer being warehoused by the publisher because of scanty sales. Orders received for out-of-print titles would go unfulfilled, and for all practical purposes the book would simply be unavailable (except for old copies that might turn up in a used bookstore). But a book whose digital files are stored at a POD facility like Lightning Source is never unavailable, because it can be printed whenever a copy is needed. This is another point that Romanos mentions: "For those titles that we didn't want to reprint, in the normal course of business you would revert the rights back to the author. But as long as Lightning was available, we could keep the title in print."

Not everyone in publishing has happily embraced the new capability of POD to ensure that no book ever goes out of print. As Romanos notes, the traditional practice has been for publishing contracts to specify that, once a book goes out of print, control of the copyright reverts to the author. When this happens, it gives the author an opportunity to make a fresh decision about what to do with the book—for example, the author might find a new publisher interested in printing a new edition, or the author might reprint the book him- or herself. Now, however, many publishers are declaring that their books never go out of print, which means, in effect, that they retain control of the copyrights in perpetuity. Groups like the Authors Guild consider this unfair to the authors whose rights they represent. They've been urging publishers to change the official definition of "in print" to specify some level of annual sales or marketing activity. However, no single solution has yet emerged to constitute a new industry standard in this area.

Time will tell how this simmering conflict will be resolved. In the meantime, publishers are benefiting from their ability to keep selling backlist titles without having to physically store copies in a warehouse. Lightning Source and POD make this possible.

By 2008, Lightning Source had over 800,000 titles in its growing digital library. That year, at a meeting of the book distributing organization Publishers

Group West in Portland, Oregon, John described how Lightning was helping to make it easier for publishers to harvest sales from the long tail of half-forgotten titles:

> I know what a missionary feels like, out in the jungle, trying to save people one at a time. And it was hard work for a long time. I'm particularly pleased that print on demand is becoming more accepted, and that more and more publishers know that its quality can be really quite exceptional. Now we can make these books in any quantity in a matter of hours. And one of the things we've learned in the process is that there's demand out there for some of your titles that you have no idea about. And if you make it easy for people to find them, you're going to be surprised at what you sell.

Mike Shatzkin is the son of Leonard Shatzkin, the book publishing expert quoted earlier in this book. Having launched his own career in partnership with his father, Mike has now become a veteran observer of the book trade in his own right. He describes the economic impact of POD on publishers this way:

> Publishers in large numbers suddenly discovered that the much simpler supply chain provided by Lightning Source was often much more effective. They could send down the book file today and have Ingram start shipping whatever quantity they need to the stores, or to Internet resellers, tomorrow. The differences in the unit costs of delivery look smaller and smaller when you see those units delivering sales that would otherwise have been lost forever. No wonder so many publishers are now submitting their content to be part of the Lightning collection. It is quite conceivable that setting up every new title at Lightning Source might become a standard routine, no matter how big or small the first printing is.

John has noted yet another benefit of the Lightning Source model for publishers. This is what he calls "just-in-case" availability—the standby capability to rapidly print any quantity of books in response to unforeseen demand for a title. In today's fast-moving world of daily news cycles and digital marketing, unpredicted bursts of consumer interest can occur any day.

One such just-in-case episode occurred in the spring of 2008 when Scott McClellan, the former press secretary to President George W. Bush, wrote an insider's account about the Bush administration, titled *What Happened*. The memoir was highly anticipated among the Washington press corps, especially when advance publicity revealed that the author, previously a Bush loyalist, had decided to use the book to air his dismay over the administration's handling of the Iraq conflict and to offer some surprising criticisms of key figures like Vice President Dick Cheney and presidential advisor Karl Rove.

The publisher—PublicAffairs, a division of the independent publisher Perseus Book Group—received large advance orders from the big bookstore chains as well as the independent booksellers. Tens of thousands of copies had actually been shipped and were ready to go on sale. But then the publicity crested, peaking when reporter Mike Allen of the widely read website Politico described the book as "scathing." More orders poured in—about eighty thousand within forty-eight hours.

PublicAffairs realized they had a potential number-one bestseller on their hands. The company immediately ordered another large offset print run, but it would take a couple of weeks to arrive. With political junkies around the country poised to descend on bookstores the moment *What Happened* was released, it would be important to find a way to replenish supplies, especially among the independent bookstores who play a vital role in creating and sustaining bestsellers. A few days with the book out of stock in key stores might kill its growing momentum.

Peter Osnos, founder and publisher of PublicAffairs, and Joe Mangan, chief operating officer of Perseus Books, sought out John Ingram. They tracked him down at a Princeton reunion and explained their problem. Lightning Source sprang into action, providing 7,500 jacketed copies to meet demand for a period of days until the larger offset run could be delivered. This rapid response helped enable the book to debut in the prestigious number-one slot on the *New York Times* bestseller list, ensuring its long-term success.

A similar episode began just a few months later, on August 29, 2008, when Senator John McCain, the Republican presidential candidate, announced that Governor Sarah Palin of Alaska would be his running mate. Palin was virtually unknown in the lower forty-eight states at the time, but reporters discovered that there was a little-known biography, titled *God, Prayer, and Sarah Palin* by Kristina Benson, that they could use as a basic source of information about the candidate. As demand for the once-obscure title suddenly spiked, depleting stocks of the existing hardcover edition, the publisher, Equity Press, contacted Ingram. Responding rapidly, the Lightning Source shop printed and shipped thousands of copies of a brand-new trade paperback edition over the course of a weekend.

Widely publicized episodes like these helped convince even more publishers of the unexpected value that could be provided by Lightning Source. Today, such just-in-case uses of POD technology are routine. After the tragic death of basketball star Kobe Bryant in a helicopter crash on January 26, 2020, publishers rushed to use Lightning Source to reprint Bryant-related books for which demand suddenly surged. A visitor to Ingram's POD facilities at the time asked a manager, "How often do opportunities like this arise?"

"Every day," was the answer.

By 2020, Ingram's fiftieth year, the Lightning Source digital library included more than eighteen million titles. This vast storehouse of content has prepared Ingram to respond to all kinds of unexpected needs. The company's so-called Guaranteed Availability Program (GAP) enables publishers to keep selling their books when traditional offset printing systems stop working.

Consider, for example, the enormous challenges posed by the 2020 COVID-19 pandemic. The dangers posed by business-as-usual during the pandemic produced unprecedented disruption to book industry supply chains. With retailers shutting down, publishing offices closing, and warehouse employees calling in sick, traditional systems for book production and distribution collapsed. Yet millions of people quarantining at home still wanted books to read; millions of kids now being home-schooled needed books to study from.

Lightning Source stepped up to fill the void. During the spring of 2020, demand for Ingram's GAP printing shot through the roof. Publishers realized that the higher per-unit cost of POD as compared with traditional, large-quantity offset printing was trivial in comparison to the risk of losing thousands of sales altogether due to the failure of traditional supply chains. In June 2020 alone, GAP printing was responsible for producing 400,000 books. In fact, for the week of June 26, five of the top ten titles on the *New York Times* nonfiction paperback bestsellers list were supplied primarily by GAP.

In October of the same year, when the American poet and essayist Louise Gluck won the Nobel Prize in literature, five of her ten titles were already in Ingram's GAP program. When the Nobel was announced, her publishers, Harper and Macmillan, quickly asked Ingram to add the other five, anticipating a sudden new demand and wanting to avoid lost sales.

It will be fascinating to observe whether, in the new post-pandemic world, reliance on POD through Lightning Source will become an even more important element of book publishers' "new normal" methods of doing business. If so, it won't be the first time that a technological breakthrough pioneered by Ingram has revolutionized the book business.

14

The Marriage Not Meant to Be

It all began with a simple question at a private meeting in a Manhattan conference room in February 1998, between Len Riggio, the chairman of Barnes & Noble, and John Ingram.

Joining them in the room were several others from each company. On the Ingram side, they included Mike Lovett (Ingram's longtime CFO and new CEO at the time), Lee Synnott, and Richard Patton, the husband of John Ingram's sister Robin. The B&N team included CEO Steve Riggio, Len's brother, and David Cully, president of distribution.

Meetings like this involving the two companies' top leaders were not unusual. The country's biggest bookstore chain and the world's largest book wholesaler generally had plenty to talk about. Ideas for specific deals were always being floated, especially by Len Riggio, whose style John describes as "free-form," "thinking out loud."

In this particular meeting, the members of the Ingram team were proposing an arrangement to provide distribution services for a Riggio-owned entity called Missouri Book Services, a textbook distributor separate from B&N. Details of a possible deal were tossed back and forth, and the resources, capabilities, needs, and goals of both the Riggio and Ingram organizations were discussed.

Both Lovett and Cully recall how, little by little, "the conversation got bigger." Cully describes what happened next:

> Len listened to everything that the Ingram team had to say. And then he turned the tables. He said, "Well, there's another way to look at this. Why don't we buy Ingram? What might be best is for us to combine the retail acumen of Barnes & Noble with the distribution acumen of Ingram. Maybe we could even slow down Amazon."

That casual-sounding comment from Len Riggio proved to be a thunderbolt that would set in motion one of the most tumultuous episodes in the history of either company.

The discussion turned concrete with surprising speed. Riggio suggested that B&N would pay $450 million for Ingram Book Group. No agreement was reached, but no one stormed out of the room, either. It was clear that both teams were intrigued by the idea of forming a permanent partnership.

In some ways, that wasn't surprising. Ingram and B&N were two of the best-run companies in any corner of the book business, filled with smart, talented people. Cully recalls his impression of the Ingram team members: "I wasn't fooled by the fact they were polite and had Southern accents. They were sneaky smart, strategically and tactically good. We used to call Lee Synnott the Grey Fox—I considered him a mentor. He taught a lot of people a lot of different things, and it was a pleasure to learn from him."

Meanwhile, Len Riggio had catapulted Barnes & Noble into the modern era, bringing intrapreneurial smarts to the challenge of transforming bookselling from an old-fashioned backwater into a high-growth, pop-culture industry. A merger of these two companies would bring together many of the most creative minds in publishing, creating a business powerhouse that would be hard to stop.

The conversation continued for another hour, with each side knowing that somehow a line was being crossed—that this day might end up being remembered as one that would change the American book business forever.

* * *

THE INGRAM DELEGATION RETURNED HOME, where they would continue the ultra-secret discussions over the next several weeks, both at corporate headquarters in Nashville and inside the executive suite of the Book Group in La Vergne.

They found the idea of selling their business to B&N, either in whole or in part, both compelling and troubling.

On the one hand, joining forces with Barnes & Noble could clarify much of the future for Ingram. Seismic changes in the publishing industry had been threatening some of the basic underpinnings of Ingram's wholesaling business. The chief threat came from the ongoing trend of consolidation. Ingram had thrived largely because of its role as a large, well-capitalized, highly efficient intermediary connecting two groups of small, numerous, relatively disorganized businesses—book publishers and book retailers. The managerial, logistical, and technological innovations that Ingram had already brought to these two groups of businesses had helped them all grow and become more profitable.

Now, however, both of these groups of businesses were rapidly consolidating. On the publisher side, the percentage of sales generated by the Big Six publishers was growing steadily as the major media conglomerates bought up proud independent publishers one by one. On the retail side, bookselling was increasingly dominated by a handful of national companies, including both the bookstore chains (led by B&N and Borders) and the rapidly growing online booksellers (overwhelmingly led by Amazon). As the many small players on both sides of the industry gave way to fewer, bigger participants, the need for Ingram as the ultra-efficient middleman came into question. More and more of the industry giants were eyeing ways to operate independently—for example, by creating their own systems for warehousing, distributing, and shipping books rather than relying on Ingram.

Thus, the evolution of the book business was challenging the strategic creativity of Ingram's leadership as never before. Partnering with B&N would be one way of resolving these issues. Ingram could emerge as a winner in the consolidation game by becoming a partner with one of the game's biggest, fiercest players.

Viewed in these terms, the deal made perfect sense. But it raised other concerns that were disturbing.

Ingram's leaders had long prided themselves on their role as neutral supporters of all parties in the publishing business. In particular, Ingram had scrupulously avoided picking sides in the war for retailing dominance. The big bookstore chains, the feisty independent stores, and other book retailers like department stores and big box discounters had all found Ingram to be friendly, valuable allies in growing their businesses.

A deal with B&N would change all that. B&N was already resented for its size and power by the independent bookstores. A partnership with Ingram was certain to be attacked by those booksellers, by trade groups like the American Booksellers Association, and by media observers who were already concerned about consolidation of ownership and control within American culture. Federal antitrust regulators might also weigh in. Ingram had bought and sold a number of businesses by this time, but it had never engaged in a transaction of this size and importance in the book industry.

Pondering these facts, the Ingram team made their first big decision: if they were to go into business with B&N, they would go in all the way. As John put it later on, reflecting on the proposed combination, "If we sold even a piece of the business to B&N, we would get 100 percent of the wrath of the independent booksellers. And so we decided that, if we were going to sell, we would sell the whole thing."

The internal conversations also raised another issue. John recalls being approached by other members of the family who asked, "How do you know there isn't somebody else that would pay you more money?"

It was a good question, and the only way to answer it was to find out. So

Ingram engaged Goldman Sachs, the international investment banking firm based in New York City, to represent Ingram in discussions with prospective buyers.

During the summer of 1998, Ingram and Goldman Sachs made formal sales presentations to three prospects. They met with leaders of the Borders bookstore chain at the company's headquarters in Ann Arbor, Michigan. They met with Jeff Bezos and other executives from Amazon at their offices in Seattle. And they spoke with Thomas Middelhoff, CEO of the German media giant Bertelsmann, and others from his team in a meeting room at Euro Disney, outside Paris, where Middelhoff was vacationing with his family. In each of these sessions, Lovett made the initial presentation, with John leading the discussion that followed. The rest of the entourage included Synnott and Mary K. Cavarra, the chief financial officer of Ingram Industries Inc.

The upshot of this process was that Barnes & Noble increased its offering price for the book group from $450 million to $600 million.

"I can't imagine that made Len very happy," John says. "But I believe the big thing Len was concerned about was whether Amazon was going to step forward and buy Ingram. It made sense for B&N to do whatever it took to keep that from happening."

In November 1998, the two companies jointly announced that B&N would acquire Ingram Content Group for $600 million in cash and stock, with the transaction qualified as "subject to regulatory review." This referred to the role of the Federal Trade Commission. The FTC review would examine any possible antitrust implications of the proposed marriage between the biggest book retailer in the United States and the country's leading book wholesaler. Technically, the B&N-Ingram deal would constitute what's called a vertical merger, combining companies that represent major players in two layers of an industry—in this case, a retailer and a wholesaler. Such mergers can be legally and economically suspect if they serve to block business channels for other participants in the industry. The FTC review process was expected to take several months, during which the sale would be on hold.

The announcement set off the expected firestorm of controversy. A memorable headline in the *Washington Post* stated, "Barnes & Noble Buys Ingram and Sets off a Powder Keg." The anger among smaller book retailers played out in many ways. Protests were lodged in both the general and trade news media, as well as at BookExpo, the annual ABA convention, held from April 29 to May 2, 1999, in Los Angeles. At the urging of indie booksellers, visitors to the vast trade show floor avoided Ingram's large booth rather than gravitating toward it as they had in past years. (Lovett says this was the first time Ingram had needed a private security detail at the convention.) The ABA itself mounted a major campaign to stop the deal. It collected over 125,000 customer signatures in a petition drive, sent letters to the FTC, and called on Congress to step in.

Ed Morrow, the Vermont bookseller and former ABA president, describes the mood of independent booksellers. He had been in the habit of reassuring them about Ingram's willingness to work cooperatively with B&N:

> I would say to them, "Don't worry about what Ingram is doing with Barnes & Noble. They are not ignoring us. They're paying attention to the needs of independents, they're perfecting those services as well." But when it looked like Ingram might be sold to B&N, that was panic time, because then this model of service was going to be owned by our competition. And all we could do was cross our fingers and pray.

The blockbuster public announcement also launched internal scrambling at Ingram in order to supply the historical and financial data required to complete the deal. Because B&N was a publicly traded company, its executives were accustomed to outside scrutiny, but Ingram now had to disclose information that had previously been regarded as highly confidential. Organizing the data was a massive job to be performed under intense time pressure.

"The amount of work that we went through as associates, making copies of anything that Legal gave us directions on, was enormous," says one veteran Ingram leader. "That lasted for about six months, and it was quite a tense time for all of us, not knowing what was going to happen from day to day."

Lovett remembers other disturbances that this period of waiting on the government regulators brought with it:

> I remember this as a time of FTC depositions, going to New York City almost weekly to meet with Len Riggio and his management team, and dealing with the 360-degree fallout with other customers, publishers, and associates—a trifecta of pain.

Lovett also suspects that the months of waiting created an opportunity for B&N's leadership to sour on the deal. John concurs, based largely on his feeling that Riggio's main goal was to keep Ingram out of the hands of Amazon. "As the deal dragged on," John says, "and it became clear that Amazon was going to build more of their own warehouses, rather than buy Ingram, I think B&N got less interested."

* * *

THE FTC STAFF KEPT ITS internal deliberations a closely guarded secret for almost seven months. No public statements were issued, and as far as the world was concerned, it appeared that the deal would go through. After all, the FTC rarely even tried to block a vertical merger attempt—and the head of the commission pointed out to a reporter from the *Times* that it had been twenty years since any such blockage had been successful in court.

But late in May 1999, the forthcoming results of the FTC review were leaked to reporters. News stories published on June 1, 1999, revealed that the FTC staff planned to recommend that the agency seek to block the purchase.

The following day was a painful one for John Ingram. He and Bill Morelli, his general counsel and one of his most trusted senior advisors within the corporation, received a series of calls starting in the middle of the morning from the Ingram company's legal team in Washington, DC. They all delivered the same message. Not only would the FTC withhold its approval of the merger, but if Ingram were to persevere in the transaction with B&N, the ensuing litigation could run for years.

FTC commissioner Sheila F. Anthony explained some of the reasoning that led her to oppose the merger in a speech to the American Bar Association almost a year later:

> Ingram is the dominant wholesaler. The gap between Ingram and the next largest wholesaler, Baker and Taylor, is very large. There were also indications that Ingram is even more important to the bookselling industry in a qualitative sense than its quantitative dominance suggests—that is, it simply does a better job of distribution. The combination of Ingram with Barnes & Noble's internal distribution center may well have increased the already high concentration in the overall book wholesaling market with the result being higher costs for retail competitors.
>
> The main vertical theory in the case was that the merger threatened to "raise rivals' costs." This theory predicted that, after the merger, Barnes & Noble could raise the costs borne by rivals such as independent bookstores and Internet retailers. Through this acquisition, Barnes & Noble would acquire the power to foreclose its retail competitors from access to an important upstream supplier.

To this day, John feels the economic and legal concerns raised by the FTC were overblown. But he also feels it was the right decision for Ingram to back down from what would have been a long, costly, and perhaps fruitless battle. "Once we knew that the FTC was going to contest the deal, that meant a trial," John says. "And while we thought the facts were strongly on our side, time was not. Given the unhappiness of the independent bookstores, it made no sense to continue going forward. And so we pulled the plug on the deal."

On June 2, Ingram and B&N issued a joint statement to the press, announcing that the proposed merger was dead.

The independent booksellers who had opposed the deal were jubilant, of course. And some other industry observers were also relieved to know that Ingram would remain independent. Jack Romanos, the chief executive at Simon & Schuster, describes his reaction this way: "I can see where it would have been of great value to B&N to have Ingram, which was the best distribution company in the business, as a division of their own company. But knowing Len's aggressiveness towards the publishers, I think it would have been a nightmare for us to have to deal with that combined entity."

For John, the death of the B&N deal was a heavy blow. He and many others within the company had dedicated long hours and absorbed plenty of criticism as they tried to make it work. Seeing all their effort go down the drain, leaving Ingram in the same place of uncertainty that had driven it into the arms of B&N in the first place, was deeply disappointing.

After absorbing the news, John stepped inside Morelli's office and closed the door. The two men sat and talked for just a few moments.

"Well, John," Morelli said, "this has been quite an experience."

"Yeah," John agreed. "And 'experience' is what you get when you don't get what you want."

"And that was the end of it," John now says. "There was no use feeling sorry for ourselves—that would have been a waste of energy. What really mattered was the next question: What the hell do we do now?"

PART FOUR
The Transformation

15

Finding New Ways to Grow

Reflecting on the collapse of the B&N deal, John Ingram says:

> My way of dealing with the disappointment was to figure out, "Okay, what do we do next?" I am much happier and more settled when I have a North Star and I'm working hard to aim myself and the organization in that general direction. I think part of our success has been that I have a bit of an innate sense about that, and then I combine it with a strong organization to help filter through the stuff I come up with that is wrong or bad. I've told people that I think our success has been based on the fact that I'm an entrepreneur inside the organization and I have a sense about things—and I think I'm usually directionally correct about it. Of course, I'm not always right. But hopefully I'm right more often than not.

At the start of the new millennium, Ingram had annual sales of over $1 billion and shipped 115 million product units a year. It was certainly not a business on the edge of collapse, or anything close to that. As John noted in one interview, "Ingram remains a strong company today with solid customer relationships and a loyal base of associates. For now, we plan to continue operating independently. We will continue to evaluate any opportunities that will help us better adapt to marketplace changes and strengthen services to our customers."

All true. But Ingram still had some serious thinking to do about what its future should be in a rapidly changing book business. The shifts roiling the industry—including both consolidation at all levels of the publishing supply chain and the increasing efforts by companies to improve their own distribution capabilities and so reduce their reliance on Ingram—would require some fresh innovation from the company's leaders.

* * *

By January 2000, following three decades of steady growth and penetration into new market segments, Ingram Book Group's total employment stood at 4,450 across all its companies and divisions. This work force was mostly deployed in eight major facilities—seven distribution centers plus a returns center—across the North American continent. But with the broader industry in a sustained period of evolutionary change, Ingram was seeing its competitive landscape transformed.

The failure of the B&N-Ingram deal sent ripples throughout the industry. Several market competitors announced adjusted plans in its wake. Baker & Taylor announced its intentions to double its own warehouse capacity. Amazon, anticipating the threat posed by a B&N-Ingram combination, had already decided to build warehouse capacity in Reno. Leaders at the ABA announced they would launch an online bookstore, called Book Sense, later in the year. And Barnes & Noble itself announced it would build a new distribution center in Memphis, Tennessee, and another in Reno, Nevada. It expected to have the facilities, each totaling approximately 350,000 square feet, online by the next summer. The company also announced a 50 percent expansion of its existing one-million-square-foot-capacity warehouse in New Jersey.

Lovett explains:

> We had wanted to keep B&N out of the distribution business. But B&N then made the strategic decision to build its own distribution center network. B&N had always been able to buy books directly from publishers for slightly less than they paid Ingram. Once they had their own distribution network, they could schedule deliveries to stores according to their own needs, and otherwise come close to duplicating the services that Ingram had been providing. The result was a large direct hit to our sales.

In response, Ingram executives began looking hard at the geographic deployment of its regional warehouses, their efficiencies and location, and how they were staffed. Their business would need to become more nimble, newly focused in its response to a changing landscape. The "new world order" of digital commerce plus changes in the physical book trade made necessary a new staffing and investment strategy. The notion of *right-sizing* now entered the company's operating vocabulary.

Reporting to John, Lovett presided over these changes as CEO. Lovett remembers the Ingram Industries board meeting in June 1999:

> The question on the table was, "What are you going to do now?" John and I said, "We are going to reinvent the Book Group." We had too

many distribution centers and too many people. As some strategy folks pointed out, it is very difficult to downsize a distribution business due to volume shortfalls, because cost-cutting involves closing distribution centers, which causes further volume losses and weakens the rest of the network. But we did in fact downsize and reorganize. And we made it work. I don't think we ever lost money, but it was tight.

Out of these discussions emerged a new topography for Ingram. What had been eight major Ingram facilities in 1997 became only four by 2004. In addition to three existing distribution centers—in La Vergne, Tennessee; Fort Wayne, Indiana; and Roseburg, Oregon—the new distribution topography included a brand-new distribution center in Chambersburg, Pennsylvania, which incorporated the operations of a nearby returns center. With 665,000 square feet of floor space, this new center had its grand opening on June 27, 2002.

Over the next decade, that four-thousand-plus head count in 2000 would prove to have been a high-water mark for staffing across the Book Group. By 2010, employment across the Book Group would shrink as the company restructured itself in order to compete and remain profitable in this new environment.

These adjustments were painful for many Ingram associates. The company provided severance assistance and also, in many cases, offers of new employment at other Ingram facilities across the United States, but of course such transfers were impractical for most of those whose jobs were eliminated. It would be another decade before Ingram's total employment returned to its pre-2000 levels.

Lovett understood the human effects of these changes on Ingram associates and their families, even as he and John and the rest of the executive team knew that this reorganizing of facilities was essential to do. "This exercise was not for the faint-hearted," Lovett recalls. "As we began the terminations, I remember saying, 'I hope we don't have to get good at this.' Later, I corrected myself. I ended up saying, 'I'm glad we got really good at this.' By which I mean that we found ways to treat everyone with as much dignity and respect as possible in difficult circumstances."

As of mid-2020, the four-location array that emerged from the restructuring remains the heart of Ingram's domestic infrastructure, together with the added capacity of a publisher distribution warehouse in Jackson, Tennessee, and extensive print-and-ship capacities at the four Lightning Source print-on-demand facilities.

Despite the reductions in staff and physical locations, Ingram's business footprint would still be national, and its delivery times to retailers would remain impressive. To remain the leader in customer service in the book industry supply chain, Ingram had to continue to provide the most titles, in the fastest manner possible, and at a price that made the most economic sense to a retail bookseller. The needed efficiency improvements were made possible by both acquisitions and technological innovations. All this would bring, in turn, new types of service and a transformation of the enterprise for a new century.

Jim Chandler would play an important role in the reinvention of Ingram. He'd grown up in southern California, where his father supervised the openings of Bank of America offices across the Golden State. After college, Jim Chandler's early career was in book retailing—first with the Pickwick Bookshops in Encino, then with the B. Dalton chain (by then part of Len Riggio's bookselling empire), later with the publisher Bantam Doubleday Dell, and then at HarperCollins. His first encounter with Ingram Book Company was during his stint at Pickwick, in the late 1970s, at an open house hosted by the Pasadena wholesaler Raymar after it was bought by Ingram in 1976. Ingram remained a presence in Chandler's career for years after that:

> For me, Ingram was always about a culture of service, going all the way back to the Raymar merger. Ingram was a lifesaver for me as a retailer. They then became even more of a lifesaver when I was in Minneapolis with B. Dalton and we ran some fairly aggressive advertising campaigns to try to counter the impact of Crown Book's discounting. Carol McIlwain, who ran Ingram's telephone sales operation in La Vergne, pulled my butt out of the fire many times, making sure that we were in stock on all the advertised titles in the various markets we served.
>
> Then, in New York with Len Riggio, we did a lot with Ingram, in terms of making certain that we could use just-in-time delivery to help counteract the impact of trying to reduce inventory holdings at a time that we were pretty heavily leveraged. That was another real lifesaver in terms of being able to manage a business with less inventory than we've had previously.

In 1997, Chandler left HarperCollins and finally joined the company that had played such an outsized role in his career to that point. His initial assignment as part of the executive team at Ingram Book Company was to grow the international exporting business, which was doing about $30 million in annual sales at the time.

"I ran international full time for about six months," Chandler recalls. "We'd set an audacious goal of tripling the business in three years, and we beat it."

Chandler was then given a succession of larger assignments, including the dual role of president of Ingram Book Company and chief commercial officer.

When the right-sizing of the distribution operations under Lovett was in full swing, Chandler became Lovett's right-hand man. This was a challenging time for Ingram, with the bookstore chains beginning to shrink; with Borders as well as B&N building their own distribution systems; and with online retailers like Amazon looking for ways to eliminate intermediaries. Chandler explains:

> To get any of this shrinking business, you had to sharpen your pencils to the point of almost no profitability. We had to have a complete breadth of inventory, systems and service that were second to none, and distribution and transportation operations of extreme efficiency. But good customer service wasn't enough. To be able to maintain our business, we needed to grow our international business, our library business, and any other areas that we could come up with. Lovett and I went through a tremendous exercise of simplifying the business, reducing the number of warehouses, enhancing transportation, and trying to grow the business anywhere we could. The whole mandate was reinvention—very solid, strategic reinvention of the business.

The Ingram team understood that merely shrinking their employee head count and eliminating distribution centers wouldn't be enough to ensure a solid future for the company. New areas of growth were essential. So Lovett, Chandler, and the rest of the team pushed hard on inventing new ways of serving Ingram's customers—both the booksellers who represented the downstream half of the book industry supply chain and the publishers who represented the upstream.

Ingram had always been adroit at working with customers on credit issues. Lovett noted that associates in the Ingram Credit Department were highly trained at assisting businesses in financial difficulties—assigning and managing credit limits, collecting past due accounts, and helping troubled customers get back on their feet. "We considered this a customer service function," Lovett says. "There aren't many better ways to help someone than to help them solve their financial difficulties."

Occasionally the challenges posed were really big ones. In 1997, the big discount bookselling chain Crown Books ran into trouble on a large scale and filed for bankruptcy while owing Ingram about $33 million. Lovett still credits Ingram's CFO Frank Kerrigan and general counsel Linda Dickert with solving that one. It took months of hard work for the Ingram team to help Crown figure out how to pay its bills while continuing to run its daily operations. Startling most observers, Ingram managed to emerge whole from the grueling process. "We collected the entire amount due plus a couple of million," Lovett says. "In Ingram lore, it's still called 'The Immaculate Collection.' I've never seen anything like it, before or since."

In later years, Ingram used its financial management expertise in support of other troubled bookselling customers. In 2001, when Borders experienced a sudden 48 percent drop in revenues, Ingram stepped in with an agreement to handle online and special sales fulfillment for the beleaguered bookstore chain. Later in the decade, with Borders deep in debt and facing the specter of bankruptcy, Ingram was for a time the only product supplier willing to do business with them. Both actions helped keep Borders afloat, its stores open, and most of the workers employed, until the chain finally entered bankruptcy in 2011. Ingram also made significant profits along the way.

Meanwhile, Ingram was also busy on the upstream part of the supply chain, seeking ways to provide valuable new services to publishers.

In 2004, Chandler invited Phil Ollila, a young executive from the Borders bookstore chain, to join his team. At Chandler's request, Ollila spent almost a year mapping a plan for an ambitious new business venture that would be called Ingram Publisher Services (IPS). Other members of Chandler's team, like Peter Clifton, then president of Ingram International, also played a role in the shaping of this plan.

The basic concept behind Ingram Publisher Services was for Ingram to become a major player in the book distribution business—that is, actively representing publishers in their efforts to sell books to retailers around the country.

The Big Six companies that dominated trade publishing didn't need such distribution services. They each had large sales forces that visited booksellers regularly, promoting upcoming books as well as active backlist titles. They also had efficient fulfillment operations that would ship books from publisher warehouses to bookstores.

But even after years of industry consolidation, there were still hundreds of smaller independent publishers that needed help with distribution. Some had made distribution deals with the Big Six publishers that let them ride on the coattails of the giant publishers in exchange for a percentage of the sales. Others worked with companies that specialized in providing book distribution services. A few of these were quite large—for example, Publishers Group West, which acted as the distribution arm for scores of small publishers, sending sales reps to bookstores across the country, fulfilling orders, and generally making sure that the pipeline connecting publishers to booksellers was flowing efficiently and profitably.

Under Phil Ollila's leadership, Ingram Publisher Services would now seek to claim a share of this business. However, it wouldn't be the first attempt by Ingram to become a player in the distribution game. As noted in chapter ten, a decade earlier Ingram had launched its Publisher Resources Inc. division, which offered fee-based distribution services for publisher clients. But PRI had been a bust. Concerned about a possible conflict between the company being in the wholesale business and PRI being a distribution business, Ingram's leadership had decided to set up PRI as a separate company, with its own information technology group, its own warehouse, its own accounting, its own administrative systems, and its own sales force. This structure created a lot of extra costs that made it almost impossible for PRI to succeed.

If IPS was to succeed where PRI had failed, it would have to avoid the mistake of reproducing the entire management, logistical, and information infrastructure of the book company. But that created its own set of challenges, as Ollila explains:

> We had to figure out how to build a separate distribution company while taking advantage of the great existing Ingram infrastructure. A lot of it was IT work, including basic stuff like defining the difference between a distribution order and a wholesale order in such a way that there could be no confusion about whom we were serving and how the costs and income were to be distributed. It was also about developing a sales force that would work alongside our wholesale sales force without conflicts or confusion.
>
> A lot of the work was the same stuff you'd do when launching any big startup company. But we had one big advantage over a typical startup, and that was Ingram's reputation. When we called a publisher and said, "We'd like you to consider making us your distribution partners," they would at least pick up the phone and listen to our pitch. Because we were Ingram.

The new business model that Ollila and his team developed made much more sense to them than the old model that PRI had followed. As Ollila observes, taking advantage of Ingram's existing infrastructure gave IPS the financial strength it needed to survive in the new publishing arena. "If you look around," he says, "there are no more distribution companies left that are pure-play distribution companies. All the ones that have survived are in a position to make use of infrastructure that is being paid for in some other way, rather than charging those huge costs to the distribution business alone. Building IPS on top of the Ingram infrastructure made it work."

It took a while to get IPS up and running. The first distribution client—Applewood Books, an independent publisher based in Massachusetts that specialized in books about American history and culture—didn't sign on until some eighteen months after the start of the project. By March 2005, when the first Applewood titles began to be shipped through IPS, a number of other small publishers had followed suit, including Bloomberg Press, the book publishing arm of the Bloomberg business media empire; Champion Press, a Toronto-based publisher of books for mental health professionals; and Make Believe Ideas, a children's book publisher with a US office in Nashville.

It so happens that the successful launch of IPS nearly coincided with a milestone in the growth of Lightning Source—namely, the posting of Lightning's first annual profit in 2004. For the smaller publishers that IPS aimed to serve, Lightning Source would be an attractive additional service. Small publishers, often serving niche audiences, loved having the ability to print books on demand, quickly and at reasonable costs, in almost any quantity needed, thereby avoiding the investment and headaches associated with producing and warehousing large volumes of physical products. Being part of the IPS distribution automatically made Lightning Source an affordable and convenient element of a small publisher's outsourcing infrastructure.

"For me," Ollila says, "one of the big questions about IPS was always, How do we create something that's different from any other distribution company? Early on, our unique selling proposition was Lightning Source."

* * *

IPS WAS JUST ONE OF several new businesses born in the early 2000s that came to characterize Ingram's redefining of itself as an important provider of services to publishers. Another was CoreSource, Ingram's digital repository, which manages and distributes content for publishers of all types.

A publisher client can upload book content to CoreSource and have it quickly, securely distributed around the world through some four hundred of the most popular channels, including Amazon Kindle, Apple Books, and Kobo. CoreSource manages format conversion processes, makes sure that consistent metadata is made available across all channels, and streamlines a multitude of other essential managerial and strategic tasks, from audit trails to analysis of sales information supplied by retailers. Providing these services leaves publishers free to concentrate on what they do best—curating or discovering valuable new content.

In its early years, however, CoreSource's road to success was bumpy. In fact, in 2009, Princeton University Press (PUP)—the distinguished publisher affiliated with John's own alma mater—unceremoniously fired CoreSource. In an urgent overnight letter to Ingram dated September 2, 2009, Peter Dougherty, director of the press, minced no words in describing his dissatisfaction:

Dear John,

I regret to inform you that after considerable deliberation we have decided to discontinue using IDG CoreSource as our digital asset management service . . . My colleagues . . . have been reporting frustration with CoreSource since we engaged them a year ago. As a result of CoreSource's persistent failure to deliver the promised services, we fear we may soon begin to lose business, if we're not already losing it.

This was big. Looking back, Dougherty thinks that sending this terse, angry letter—rather than starting with a simple complaint delivered through ordinary channels—was "kind of a foolish thing." But it worked. John Ingram called Dougherty immediately. "I was so shocked, I had to pick myself up off the floor," he says. Ingram assured Dougherty that he would respect the press's decision and do everything necessary to facilitate a smooth transition to another service provider. "But first," he said, "I ask you to give us another chance."

"This was on a Friday afternoon," Dougherty recalls. "The next Monday, John had a guy waiting for me when I showed up at the front door of the press offices at eight-thirty in the morning." That guy was John Campbell, a six-foot, eight-inch Harvard grad who'd been sent by Ingram to work on PUP's problems. Campbell, in turn, was working under the supervision of Shawn Morin, who'd been on the job as Ingram's chief technical officer for all of two weeks.

Morin had brought an unusual resume when he joined Ingram. He had previously worked on guidance systems for NASA's space shuttle program. Then he'd headed information technology management for a number of consumer goods companies, including Bass Pro Shops, the large outdoor products retailer. John had brought him to Ingram to help build the technical systems needed for the company's next phase of growth.

But soon after his arrival, Morin found that his first challenge was to bring Ingram's existing systems up to date. "On my first day," he recalls, "I walked into the data center and saw that the doors were propped open and fans were blowing to keep the machinery cool. I thought, 'Uh-oh, I should've seen this before I took the job.'"

The problems with PUP's CoreSource service were emblematic of the problems Morin faced. "Ingram had bought a software package that couldn't handle the volume," Morin explains. "They were running it on old hardware that they hadn't kept up to date, so it was falling down. I shut down all sales, which made everybody lose their minds for a while. But I had to do it."

Morin used a simple diagram to explain to his new Ingram team why it was necessary to take such a drastic step:

> I drew a pyramid, and I said, "This pyramid represents our data systems. There are three layers to this pyramid. The bottom layer is the foundation. The second layer is value-add. And the tip of the pyramid is competitive advantage. The problem is that everybody wants to play in the top two layers. But if you don't have the foundation right, the pyramid is going to tip over or collapse. That's where we are right now."
>
> You know, if you're a technology startup with a bright idea, customers may give you some leeway. They'll put up with a glitch or two. But we're held to a different standard. If you're Ingram, people expect it to work.

Morin and Campbell collaborated for several weeks on fixing PUP's CoreSource problems. In the process, they learned more about the underlying weaknesses of Ingram's IT infrastructure. Those lessons served Morin and his other team members well as they worked on rebuilding that infrastructure virtually from scratch.

The second chance that Dougherty granted to Ingram turned out well for both organizations. PUP's retooled CoreSource system ended up providing excellent service to the publisher, and John was restored to the good graces of his alma mater. In fact, several years later, Dougherty invited him to be the kick-off speaker at an internal session focused on how to prepare Princeton University Press for future changes in the publishing industry. Ingram calls that invitation "a moment of redemption." Exhibiting a touch of self-deprecating humor, he kicked off his presentation by showing a copy of the Dougherty letter firing him, followed by a Virginia Slims cigarette ad with the slogan, "You've Come a Long Way, Baby."

Sometimes, what looks like a business disaster can be turned into a wake-up call—provided you respond in the right way. With the foundation solidly rebuilt, CoreSource was ready to serve as the flagship for a whole fleet of Ingram businesses specializing in valuable services to publishers—the new arena of growth that John Ingram had been seeking.

16

"Not My Father's Ingram"

In September 2005, a new entity called Ingram Digital Ventures was formed within the evolving Ingram structure. The mission of IDV would be to identify promising acquisition opportunities from among the many new ventures emerging in the digital realm around the world.

John Ingram asked Mike Lovett to serve as president and CEO of this highly focused hunting party. It would operate quietly. Lovett, in turn, invited four men onto his elite leadership team. Kent Freeman, the veteran Ingram executive and computer systems specialist, would become the chief information and technology officer. Andrew Weinstein would coordinate business development. David Roland, who had been a legal officer in the content group, would now head up mergers and acquisitions for IDV. And Jim Nye, a former executive with the independent publisher John Wiley, was recommended by Jim Chandler to be the new coordinator for education programs.

In keeping with its guarded public profile, the IDV team set up shop in the rear of Ingram Building 14 in La Vergne, initially sharing some space with a noon yoga group. It was understood that, eventually, when the time was right, the digital businesses built by IDV would be unified with Lightning Source as part of the Book Group or a successor entity, though this was not generally broadcast at the time, lest such ambitions become unnecessarily disruptive within the existing Ingram organization.

Operational planning for IDV began in January 2006, during a day-long retreat at the Marriott Hotel in Franklin, Tennessee, some thirty miles from the Ingram campus in La Vergne. The new team worked out its operating mode, identified its target digital markets, and devised a one-page operating plan as well as a one-page systems plan for internal and board use.

The team immediately set to work building a collection of new digital businesses, largely through acquisitions. "We didn't have the time to build a digital business from scratch that could be in all the markets we thought we needed to be in," Lovett recalls. "We didn't have the resources—particularly the talent—or the digital content experience to do that. The only exception was CoreSource, our digital warehouse repository. That was in the Ingram sweet spot from our experiences at Ingram Book Group and Lightning Source.

CoreSource became part of the IDV portfolio. We also migrated to IDV the retail ebook business that we'd started at Lightning Source."

The first acquisition prospect that the IDV team focused on was VitalSource Technologies (VST), located in Raleigh, North Carolina. VST had been launched in 1994 after a professor in the school of dentistry at the University of Texas at San Antonio noticed that students were not buying all the books they needed. The high cost of textbooks was a big part of the problem. His solution was to develop an ebook digital platform with sophisticated content and search capabilities specifically designed to serve the needs of students. The business was acquired by a group of investors in Raleigh led by Frank Daniels III, whose family had previously been longtime owners of Raleigh's daily newspaper.

Building on the dental training business base, VST soon expanded into nursing education and then into other educational arenas. It developed into one of the most advanced digital content businesses at the time. The VST programming team developed a unique set of content markup tools—technically known as a document type definition (DTD)—that provided publishers with a broader range of media options and searchability capabilities than the current book industry standards for electronic publishing. VST employed these tools to manage digital file conversions for its publisher clients, using a server in India to house its software and content.

By the mid-2000s, VST had a solid management team but needed capital to grow further. The IDV team recognized the company as a logical acquisition. Lovett recalls, "It was one of those infrequent times in business when you knew nearly immediately that this was a fit. VST had talent and competencies but was hamstrung by a lack of funds. Ingram needed VST's capabilities, had its own complementary skills, had market presence and access, and had a disciplined successful corporate structure, plus financial resources."

VST also fit beautifully into the emerging vision of Ingram as a broad-based provider of services to the publishing industry, with its feet firmly planted in both the traditional print world and the emerging digital world. VST's Frank Daniels, who would become an executive at Ingram, is credited with a memorable observation that IDV's leaders would later embrace. When asked whether ebooks might eventually replace printed textbooks, Daniels would say, "The future will be an either/and world, not an either/or world." He was right.

In July 2006, VitalSource joined the portfolio of digital businesses positioning Ingram to help lead the transition to that either/and world.

The next acquisition target identified by Andrew Weinstein was MyiLibrary, a digital content business in the academic library market. James Gray, the owner of MyiLibrary, also owned Coutts Information Services, a print book distribution business serving the academic library market, which Ingram found attractive. In December 2006, Gray sold the two businesses to Ingram. He then joined the company as CEO of the expanding new division now called Ingram Digital Group (IDG), which had already grown to include over two hundred associates in three countries on two continents.

IDG continued to add other businesses to its portfolio. It entered the smartphone digital content arena through an investment in Mobifusion, a California-based app distributor, and obtained a foothold in the world of intellectual property management through a number of joint projects with a Virginia-based defense contractor known as Blackbird Technologies.

Of course, the other big digital business at Ingram was Lightning Source, which continued to grow throughout the 2000s. In July 2002, J. Kirby Best was named president of Lightning Source, and for several years he managed its growth successfully. Under Best's leadership, Lightning's digital library continued its dramatic growth, and its printing capabilities were enhanced, including the addition of a hardcover binding option and the ability to print book interiors in full color. These allowed Lightning to begin producing impressive photo books designed using consumer-friendly, do-it-yourself software.

Ingram's other digital initiatives of the mid-2000s would open doors to new applications for both Lightning Source and Ingram Publisher Services. But taking full advantage of these new opportunities would require improvements in the management and coordination of those systems for maximum efficiency and productivity.

The earliest manifestation of this was in the need to better integrate the book manufacturing tasks at Lightning Source with the work of the Book Group's distribution system and logistics capabilities. With the POD business booming and taking on growing importance in Ingram's future, it was time to take a new look at Lightning Source's place within Ingram Book Group. The two operations did not work together effectively. "In effect, there was a virtual wall between them," John remembers.

> The book company would throw orders over the wall to Lightning. Lightning would take the orders, make the books, come back to the wall, and throw the books over to the book company. It was just sub-optimal, with wasted paperwork, energy, money, and time. We needed to tear down the wall and truly merge the two operations, with no artificial barrier. Doing that would take hours out of the manufacturing process.

John's explanation vividly illustrates how the book business had been transformed by digitization. A generation earlier, book publishers had been content to rely on a distribution system that required retailers on the West Coast to wait *weeks* for books to arrive from warehouses in the East. Now the supply chain had become so efficient that cutting hours out of the delivery process was important enough to justify a corporate reorganization.

After many planning sessions, John and his team decided to bring Lightning Source more fully inside the consolidated organization of the Book Group. Once this shift was accomplished, both Lightning Source and the new digital businesses would reside alongside the book wholesaling business. But this internal realignment took longer to accomplish than anyone expected.

Cultural differences were one of the main reasons. From its founding, Lightning Source had been separated from the broader Ingram organizational structure, with its traditional practices and procedures. "The Lightning folks took a lot of pride in their operation," John explains. "They were the smart technology experts, not the sleepy old 'yesterday' company. So putting them together wasn't easy. I didn't want to blow up what was good about Lightning. But it was clearly time to make the move."

In 2009, the Ingram Content Group (ICG) was formed by the merger of Ingram Book Group with Ingram Digital Group. Soon thereafter, Kirby Best was relieved of his duties at Lightning Source. He'd produced a lot of value for Ingram, but he never got comfortable with the move to combine his operation with the larger operation. At the same time, David "Skip" Prichard was named CEO of the combined group.

Full integration of Lightning with the rest of Ingram's services continued to pose challenges for the organization. The essential issue was the pace of change in an industry that was still transitioning to a new normal. John was pushing the executives who reported to him to think big about the opportunities emerging all around them. "I didn't want us to settle for 5 percent growth," John recalls. "I felt we could reach for growth that would be transformational, not just incremental."

Under the circumstances, Skip Prichard felt it was best for him to pass the leadership torch. "John had a vision that he wanted to realize," Prichard has said. "It was his vision, so it made sense for him to carry it out." When Prichard departed in June 2012, John stepped into the CEO role.

For the first time in memory, the book business had become a hot territory. "Amazon was making headlines and transforming the industry with its Kindle," John explains.

Then Apple jumped into the fray with its iPad. Suddenly the book business had morphed from being a sleepy, old-fashioned backwater into the latest battleground of the tech revolution. Venture capital firms looking for big new opportunities began circling the world of publishing. It was an amazing time. And we realized that, if Ingram was going to take full advantage of these new opportunities, we needed to start thinking like venture capitalists—looking for great little startups with the potential to add value to our existing service offerings or to create brand-new ones.

John asked Roland to take on this new assignment. Reporting directly to John and Morin, Roland shifted from focusing on mergers and acquisitions to help design another new entity called ICG Ventures, whose mission would be the identification of strategic business acquisition prospects for the company. From this initiative came a number of businesses that would develop under the Ingram corporate umbrella. In time, this would bring into the Ingram family of companies a number of diverse new business activities, each focused on enhancing Ingram's services to publishers and others in the book industry.

One of these companies was Aerio, a service originally created by Ron Martinez, a former Yahoo! executive and founder of a San Francisco–based company called Invention Arts. Aerio offered an array of online tools that publishers, retailers, and authors could use to market and sell books, whether in print or digital form. Among other capabilities, Aerio made it easy to sell books through any website, blog, or social media presence; it provided social marketing services to help promote books to readers—for example, by enabling customers to download a free book chapter as an inducement to buy; it offered simple tools to let even novice retailers and marketers create attractive online product catalogs, including video, audio, and images; and it enabled retailers to have immediate access to millions of books and other products from Ingram's own virtually limitless catalog.

In effect, Aerio made it possible for anyone with the desire to do so to become an online bookseller, quickly and easily. This made it a natural, compelling complement to other services Ingram offered, especially the POD capabilities of Lightning Source, which had already made it possible for anyone with a manuscript to become a publisher. In December 2015, Ingram acquired Aerio. It has continued to expand and diversify the business's service offerings ever since, growing from a $5-to-$10-thousand-per-month business to a $50 thousand one.

A second ICG Ventures catch was Verba, a San Francisco–based company that had originated in a student government project created by three students at Harvard. Its goal: to make textbooks more affordable by using technology tools to make prices more transparent, streamline the creation of customized electronic course materials, and help campus stores make books more accessible for all students. By the time Ingram acquired Verba in April 2017, it had built collaborations with more than 350 college and university bookstores, and was serving over three million students each term.

Yet another digital acquisition by Ingram was OptiQly, a New York–based startup cofounded by a former publishing executive named Evan Schnittman and a group of partners that included Mike Shatzkin, the consultant quoted earlier. OptiQly's business was built to help publishers make sense of the flood of new customer and sales data being created by online sales tools like Amazon as well as social media sites like Facebook and Twitter. Publishing consultant Cliff Guren explained how it worked in a blog post describing the company's partnership with Ingram:

> OptiQly aggregates over 50 data points from Amazon's web pages, Goodreads, Facebook, Twitter and Wikipedia for every book in the Amazon marketplace. The aggregated data is used by their proprietary algorithms to calculate two scores for each title: Product Authority and Brand Authority. The Product Authority score reflects how well the book is optimized for discovery and sale. The Brand Authority score reflects the extent to which the author-focused marketing on the Amazon site and on the Web contributes to discovery and sale. The Product and Brand Authority scores are then combined to produce an "OQ" (OptiQly) score that shows how well the whole marketing effort for a given title is optimized for discovery and sale on Amazon's platform.

In a world where old-school publishers were struggling to realize the potential value in the new online tools for selling, marketing, and promoting books, OptiQly promised to offer a helping hand—a digital variation on the kind of publisher support service that Ingram had long been famous for providing. Ingram announced an investment in OptiQly in June 2017, when the company's service was in the beta testing phase; in November of the same year, Ingram acquired OptiQly's assets in full.

* * *

The death of Bronson Ingram in June 1995 and the leadership transition that followed had led to a transformation of the family business. Ingram had morphed from a traditional book wholesaler into a provider of a complex new suite of multiple services to book retailers, publishers, authors, and more. The rise of Lightning Source had foreshadowed this remarkable shift. Later, the demise of the Barnes & Noble deal had added urgency to the need to redefine Ingram's role in a rapidly changing industry, helping to spur the company's leaders to accelerate the shift.

To understand the complexity and the scale of this transformation, consider two corporate documents published in the Ingram company newsletter in March 1998. The first is a "conversation" with Orrin Ingram and John Ingram, co-presidents of the parent company, describing the corporate culture of Ingram Industries.

Question: How would you define the "new" Ingram Industries Inc. today?

Answer: Some companies define themselves in terms of one single business idea. For example, Sony defines itself in terms of "miniaturization," and Honda defines itself as a designer of motors. Ingram Industries is not like that. We are much more a group of core businesses.

Question: What does "core" mean?

Answer: "Core" means businesses where we have scale, competitiveness, staying power/sustainability in the areas where we do business. We are also a family business. Two of the keys for any family to be successful are:

1. The family needs to get along. We certainly do.

2. The family needs to have feelings for—and identify with—its businesses. We certainly do.

Question: I hear a lot about "corporate culture" in business these days. How would you describe the "corporate culture" of Ingram Industries?

Answer: We believe our corporate culture at Ingram has seven important aspects:

1. First and foremost, the company must continue to operate with the highest degree of integrity.

2. We want Ingram Industries to be a fun, innovative and creative place to work.

3. We support a collaborative team-focused environment. Someone has to be responsible for making decisions, and as co-presidents of the company we don't shy away from this. We believe we will reach the best answers by fostering a non-dictatorial and participatory type of environment.

4. Our associates must be customer-focused. We only exist because of our customers.

5. We must operate with a sense of urgency. We have to move fast to stay ahead of our customers' expectations.

6. We have to stay flexible, nimble and situational.

7. Finally, we want to be developers of associates. One of the greatest satisfactions that can be achieved is watching others grow and succeed.

The second document was a corporate mission statement, which appeared on the same page of the newsletter.

Our Mission

Ingram Book Group is a distribution industry leader and innovator. Our primary objective is to develop the people and organization necessary to provide the fastest, most efficient and accurate wholesale distribution services to our customers. In so doing, we intend to be the preeminent distributor in our chosen market segments. We will deliver maximum value to our customers by providing superior distribution performance with less invested time and capital than our competition. We have earned the highest respect of our customers and suppliers, and we will always be committed to living up to our reputation. We will provide our Ingram associates with a challenging, growth-oriented, secure working environment in which they may develop personally and professionally. We are committed to supporting the communities where our associates work and live.

Our mission: To lead the industry in customer service.

Taken together, these two documents described Ingram in admirably clear terms. They defined Ingram's main business objectives and described the kind of corporate culture that Ingram's leaders believed had contributed to the company's long-term success, as well as making it a place where people *liked* to work. And perhaps most notably, they depicted the business in terms that could well have been used to describe it as far back as the 1960s, when Ingram first dipped its toe into the book business.

Now compare this vision of Ingram with the very different one painted by John just a decade later. Again, two documents help tell the tale.

The first is a speech given by John in November 2008, in Portland, Oregon. It was the keynote address before the annual meeting of PubWest, the trade association of publishers, booksellers, and related industry executives from across the Pacific Northwest.

John's goal was to help his audience understand the transition that his family business had been navigating. He respectfully titled his talk "It's Not My Father's Ingram," and it provided the template for similar speeches that he would give to other trade groups as well as to multiple meetings within the Ingram companies.

"As much as it's not my father's Ingram," he began, "I would say, in a more generalized sense, that the publishing industry today is not our fathers' publishing industry." He continued:

> It's difficult to believe, but I certainly believe that the pace of change has gotten faster than it was even nine months ago, and nine months ago, quite frankly, seems like an eternity . . . And so as we've gotten into 2008, we've seen more changes. We've seen Sony getting into electronic publishing. We've seen Apple with its whole application store. But a lot of the questions from 2007 are still the right questions to be asking—like, how do I take some of the new ideas and new technologies and convert them into reality? How do I determine where to invest in order to drive the best outcomes for my publishing company? How do I innovate, and how do I create the change?
>
> It may be helpful to take a step back and look more closely at certain things that have and haven't changed. And I want to do that with regard to my father's Ingram. Because, while the Ingram that I live in today is not my father's Ingram, there are a lot of qualities that were important to the traditional business that we still have, and are still important parts of our business today. Things like efficient, reliable distribution. Speed. Selection. Choice. Fulfillment across lots of different channels. And being a trusted partner.
>
> These qualities, in my opinion, are just as important today as they were forty years ago, if not maybe more so . . . So today's Ingram is not

my father's Ingram, but a lot of the needs that exist in the marketplace are the same, and it's just that the complexity of dealing with them has increased exponentially. If you talk about efficient, reliable distribution, the basic need is the same as ever. But the methods of distribution are evolving.

In this keynote address, Ingram carefully balanced change with continuity, as if to assure his listeners that the torrent of innovation sweeping their old, tradition-laden industry wouldn't lessen his company's commitment to the values that had made it great—and that had helped so many in his audience thrive.

A similar instinct for striking a healthy balance between seemingly conflicting drives may inform one of John's favorite in-house mantras: "Let's be brave, not stupid." It's a slogan John invokes when his team is wrestling with a decision about some proposed innovation. Is this idea an example of bold, ambitious thinking fueled by an appropriate sense of urgency? Or does it cross the line into taking needless risks without a reasonable hope of reward? "Let's be brave, not stupid" is John's way of helping people zero in on the correct answer in regard to any single decision. It's the sum of those decisions, of course, that shape the larger long-term destiny of any company.

And in different venues, John's way of striking the balance between bravery and stupidity, change and continuity, may sometimes differ. Just a few months after his keynote speech, in a June 2009 interview in *Publishers Weekly*, he gave significantly greater stress to the need for change. He began by describing how the appearance of Stephen King's ebook *Riding the Bullet* in 2000 had been a wake-up call:

> At that moment, it brought the thought that digital distribution was going to explode on the scene. I had to make a call to put a lot more money toward it. While it took a few more years for digital books to begin taking off, those initial investments laid the groundwork for Ingram Digital. We kind of bumped along with digital until 2005 or so when it just seemed that it was starting to happen. 2005 was when it became clear that digital was coming back . . .
>
> Publishers are really quite busy just managing the traditional business they've had, and not too many of them have got a bunch of extra capital to come up with their own proprietary digital solutions. All of them need to be looking at digital as a threat *and* an opportunity. We live in a world that we call an "either/and" world, not "either/ or." Customers want physical goods in some circumstances, digital in

others. It's a daunting task to figure out how to provide that, when your core business is trying to figure out how to shepherd the creation of content.

John went on to declare, "Ingram is a more valuable resource to publishers today than at any time in our history." He had solid grounds for making this bold claim. Over the previous two decades, the company had developed comprehensive services to support both the physical and the digital sides of publishing. The company's willingness to embrace dramatic change—and its readiness to help participants in every sector of the book industry navigate that change successfully—had become central to John's leadership, both inside and outside the family business.

He drove home the message of transformational change in every speech, every interview, every letter to shareholders, and even through some remarkable symbolic gestures. For example, there was the time, in November 2013, when John strode to the lectern at a sales meeting of Ingram Content Group dressed in the helmet and battle gear of the robotic character Optimus Prime, an extraterrestrial being featured in the Transformers franchise of comics, video games, and cartoons. Doffing the helmet, he introduced himself as "Ingramus Prime" and proceeded to deliver yet another heartfelt speech about the importance of transformation.

"I wanted to do something impactful," John recalls with a laugh. "Not only about my desire, but also about my commitment to making sure we stayed relevant. I think the costume helped make the point."

* * *

JOHN'S LIGHT-HEARTED FORAY INTO the world of cosplay surely got the attention of his Ingram associates. His speeches and other public messaging about transformation gave further weight to the importance of the theme. But the most powerful evidence of John's commitment to retooling his family business for the twenty-first century came in the concrete business decisions he'd made for more than a decade—decisions that embodied the intrapreneurial mantle he'd taken on after his father's death.

Looking back, we can identify a series of classic intrapreneurial moves that John made over those years of change. They included:

- Asking provocative questions (like "Why are we wallpapering our warehouse?") to challenge age-old business assumptions, and then being bold enough to follow the answers no matter where they might lead.

- Giving innovative managers the freedom and the resources to try brand-new strategies and business models (like print-on-demand publishing), even when the long-term payoff was far from guaranteed.
- Having the honesty to recognize when the business model on which you've built your success is approaching its sell-by date—and the decisiveness to pivot to a new model before it's too late.
- Being flexible enough to use a variety of tactics in the pursuit of growth, including building new businesses from scratch, investing in promising ideas from outside the company, hiring impressive talent from other firms and even from other industries, and buying entire organizations when the timing and the price were right.
- Having the wisdom to recognize and retain what is most valuable and enduring about the corporate culture you've inherited (like Ingram's heritage as a customer-centric, service-oriented organization) while also recognizing when change is essential to retain your relevance in a new era.

Ingram Content has been blessed by a succession of gifted leaders, each of whom made unique contributions to sustaining and enhancing the company's ongoing success. John Ingram has played his part in turning his "father's Ingram" into a powerhouse of technological innovation brilliantly suited for success in an era unlike any that previous generations could have imagined.

17
Ingram and the World

Ingram now inhabits much of the globe, its business footprint no longer national but international, with operations on five continents. Over the past two decades, a combination of technological adaptation, business model innovation, team building, and far-seeing strategy—all built on a foundation of superlative customer service—has enabled Ingram to expand successfully across Canada, Europe, the Middle East, South America, Asia, and Australia.

By January 2020, across all its divisions, Ingram Content Group employed over four thousand associates, the largest head count in its history. These associates are engaged in providing a long and ever-expanding list of sophisticated services to publishers large and small; booksellers of every description; public, academic, and corporate libraries; educational institutions at every level; and growing numbers of authors, both traditional writers affiliated with commercial or nonprofit presses and self-publishing authors who use Ingram's tools to reach audiences of readers directly.

In addition to the corporate headquarter sites in La Vergne and Nashville, Tennessee, Ingram domestic operations are found today in New York City, Boston, San Francisco, Berkeley, Fresno, Minneapolis, Raleigh, and Seattle; in Chambersburg, Pennsylvania; Ft. Wayne, Indiana; Roseburg, Oregon; and Antioch and Jackson, Tennessee. Ingram Publisher Services and Lightning Source have international facilities in London, Plymouth, and Milton Keynes in the United Kingdom; in Maurepas, France; in Rosenheim, Germany; and in Melbourne, Australia.

More international operations are now in the works. In November 2019, Ingram reached an agreement with Sheikh Dr. Sultan bin Muhammad al-Qasimi, the ruler of Sharjah, to build a POD facility at Sharjah Publishing City in the United Arab Emirates. This complex of offices, warehouses, and manufacturing plants will serve the book industry throughout the Middle East, North Africa, and India. Billed as "the world's first free trade zone for publishing," Publishing City is also a tax-free haven for freedom of the press that will hopefully help bring new creativity and energy to the region's cultural life.

* * *

INGRAM'S GROWING NETWORK OF INTERNATIONAL connections has opened up some important domestic opportunities. Perhaps the most significant example emerged from an acquaintance between two men—David Taylor, a Brit with the soul of a booklover and the charm of a born salesman, and Arnaud Nourry, a one-time consulting engineer who'd ended up heading the French company Hachette, one of the world's great publishers.

Taylor had begun his career in the book trade on the shop floor at Blackwell's, the famous bookstore in Oxford. During his fourteen years with Blackwell's, he ended up running the company's global library supply business while also running his own Internet-based sales business, working with clients that included George Soros's foundation. In 2003, Taylor was invited to join Lightning Source in the UK to help deepen and expand Ingram's reach into the British market. There, he worked with Suzanne Wilson-Higgins, the commercial director for Lightning Source UK, who had also worked previously for Blackwell's.

"The big challenge," Taylor recalls, "was that nobody in the book trade really understood what Lightning Source did. The marketing material at the time was very technical. I said to John Ingram, 'It's a brilliant product, a brilliant service, but for God's sake let's put it in language that the book trade uses rather than technical language.'"

Taylor used his long list of contacts in the British publishing industry to energize Lightning Source UK's marketing efforts. He eventually became the company's managing director.

It was a 2007 conversation between Taylor and his friend David Young, another experienced British publishing professional, that led to a connection between Ingram and Hachette. "I happened to be in New York," Taylor remembers, "and I called in to see David, who had recently started with Hachette in the United States." Young had previously toured Ingram's Lightning Source operation in Tennessee, and he'd been impressed by its innovation potential. Now the two friends hatched a further plan:

> David suggested that his boss, Arnaud Nourry, soon to become chairman of Hachette Livre, should come and visit Tennessee to see the Lightning Source operation. POD was almost unknown in the French market at that time. Arnaud happened to be coming to the United States, so we fixed up an Ingram plane to collect him for the visit. John Ingram had never met Arnaud, and he was excited to hear that he was going to come and visit Ingram.

Nourry didn't know very much about Ingram. "I was not exposed to the American market that much," Nourry remembers.

> I was very Europe-centric. I guess in the first one or two years after Hachette began investing in the United States, I learned that Ingram was a wholesaler for small accounts, libraries, and a few mass merchandisers, and also a print-on-demand provider. I knew who they were, but I did not have a lot of contact with them.

However, Nourry quickly realized the potential value of POD for Hachette: "We had an extremely long list of titles in France. A lot of them were not moving in any significant quantities on a yearly basis, and, as a result, many were going out of print. A print-on-demand facility could solve that problem for us."

The meeting between Nourry and Ingram led to plans for a joint venture between Ingram and Hachette that they would call Lightning Source France. It would include a new, state-of-the-art printing operation at Hachette's distribution facility outside Paris. "It took us a while to put together the joint venture," Nourry says.

> This was quite bold on John's part, because, for an American company of Ingram's size, investing in France was not entirely natural. I guess the size of Hachette and the personal relationship we had started building were the reasons why he considered our proposal a serious one. It took us a few months to incorporate the company. Then we started building the business from scratch, buying the machines and winning support from French publishers both inside and outside the Hachette group.
>
> It took about five years for the joint venture to break even, which was more or less what we had anticipated. It's been nicely profitable since. We've invested in new machines when needed. We're expanding, and we're doing extremely well.

Today, Lightning Source France has digital files for about 100,000 book titles, ships around a million units every year, and serves fifteen thousand retailers around the world. The prestigious partnerships the company has developed include an arrangement with the National Library of France—the equivalent of our Library of Congress—whereby Lightning Source France works with retailers to market out-of-print books from the library's online collection, known as Gallica.

This new business operation in France has been a significant addition to Ingram's global portfolio. But even more important, the growing friendship between John and Nourry helped open the door for a lucrative US business opportunity for Ingram. It came about as a result of Hachette's ongoing effort to expand its publishing presence in the United States.

As we've seen, the American publishing scene had been increasingly dominated by international conglomerates like Germany's Bertelsmann and Britain's HarperCollins. The French Hachette joined this trend. By the mid-2010s, Hachette had acquired such respected American publishers as Little, Brown and Warner Books (the latter now renamed Grand Central Publishing) and was publishing about twelve hundred books in the United States annually.

As he scanned the horizon for additional acquisition opportunities, Nourry was attracted to one of the best independent publishers—the Perseus Book Group. Founded in 1996 by investor Frank Pearl, Perseus had grown into a $100 million publisher with such well-known imprints as Basic Books, Da Capo Press, Nation Books, and PublicAffairs. It was an especially interesting opportunity for Nourry because Hachette's US business was dominated by fiction and frontlist titles. By contrast, Perseus was best known for publishing serious nonfiction books with significant backlist sales potential. Acquiring Perseus would help bring greater balance to Hachette's US portfolio.

Nourry set about negotiating a deal with David Steinberger, the president and publisher of Perseus, and the company's owners, an investment firm called Centre Lane Partners. A tentative agreement reached in 2014 fell apart. But two years later, the two companies returned to the bargaining table, and this time they succeeded.

The deal they negotiated was inevitably a complex one. Perseus was really two companies. In addition to its publishing arm, Perseus owned a big book distribution business, which included the well-known company Publishers Group West. Serving some six hundred small publishers, this distribution business generated about $300 million in annual revenue for Perseus. It was a large, profitable business—but not one that Hachette was interested in. They were busy enough developing a distribution operation to serve their growing US publishing operations; taking on distribution for thousands of additional titles every year would have overwhelmed them.

Fortunately, Nourry had a solution: "It took me all of thirty seconds after I finished my negotiations with David Steinberger to call John Ingram."

Perseus's distribution business may not have been attractive for Hachette, but it was a perfect fit for Ingram. As you recall, back in 2004, Ingram had jumped into the distribution business through its launch of Ingram Publisher Services (IPS).

Since then, IPS had expanded steadily but slowly, building a portfolio of about one hundred publisher clients. Taking on the Perseus distribution clients would bring a massive jolt of growth. It would have taken decades for IPS to attract six hundred new publisher clients one at a time; now they would join the fold in one fell swoop.

Hachette and Ingram quickly made a financial deal. Hachette kept Perseus's publishing operations; Ingram bought the distribution business.

Then began a lengthy, complicated job of making the handover work. "I can tell you that separating the various parts of an existing business is a very complex undertaking," Nourry says. "You have to duplicate the IT, the infrastructure, I mean everything. It takes a lot of professionalism, trust, and even friendship to be able to work it all out." This instant expansion of Ingram's distribution business had a major impact on the overall strategic shape of the organization. In John's words, "The center of gravity for Ingram Content Group shifted from wholesale to publisher services with the Perseus acquisition."

For Ingram's bottom line, the shift to publisher services has been a significant advance. A simple graph presented at an Ingram board meeting in 2017 told the tale (see Figure 17-1). It demonstrated how Ingram Content Group had grown its profits dramatically over the most recent twenty-five years, with a growing share coming from Ingram's broadening of its publisher services segment. The title of the graph probably said it best: *Innovation Drives the Business.*

* * *

MEANWHILE, AS INGRAM WAS INNOVATING on a grand scale—entering partnerships with publishing giants like Hachette and organizing distribution networks to serve hundreds of publishers—it was also transforming the craft of book publishing on the smallest possible scale: one copy at a time. Here's an illustrative story.

In 2018, Ed Morrow, the prominent Vermont bookseller, phoned John with a special request. Morrow's sister, an artist and writer named Jane Trigère, had been diagnosed with cancer and was declining very fast. She'd decided to forgo chemotherapy and was quietly preparing for a peaceful death at home. Every couple of days, Morrow would take the hour-and-forty-five-minute drive to visit her there.

In their conversations, Trigère expressed only a few regrets about the looming end of her life. Perhaps the biggest was the fact that she'd never been able to publish a book for children that she'd written and illustrated. Titled *What's a Grandparent?*, it was about the joys of being a grandparent, dedicated

Innovation Drives the Business
Ingram Content Group Profit, Legacy vs. New Services

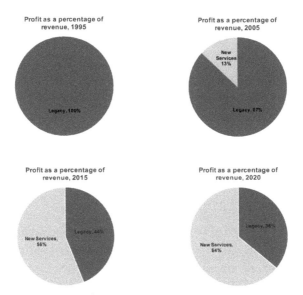

An earlier version of this graphic, shown at an Ingram board meeting in 2017, dramatized the impact of the new service business on the company's income stream In 2005, the profit split between legacy business and new services business had been 87:13. By 2020, the ratio had changed to 64:34. In other words, Ingram's new suite of services for publishers had grown to generate almost two-thirds of the company's annual profits.

to Trigère's teenage grandson, and she'd completed all the drawings but one. She'd even worked with a book designer on laying out the pages. But now it looked as though time would run out before her dream of authorship could be fulfilled.

"John," Morrow asked, "I'm afraid Janie may not be with us much longer. Can you help?"

Just a few minutes later, Morrow got a call from Craig Pollock, a manager with Lightning Source. A Philadelphia native, Pollock had been a bookseller in the Miami area before joining Ingram in 1992. His family had owned Bookworks, an independent store in Coral Gables, Florida, and were among the early organizers of the Miami Book Fair, together with Mitch Kaplan, owner of Books & Books. All were active in the Southeast Booksellers Association.

"Ed, what do you need?" Pollock asked.

The two men talked through the state of Trigère's book project, and Pollock explained the kind of computer file he would need to turn it into a finished product. "Send it to me as quickly as possible, and we'll turn it around overnight," Pollock said.

Within a few days, Trigère's dream had come true. The printed book, filled with her colorful illustrations, arrived in the mail. "We were able to show the book to Janie and read it to her," a grateful Morrow remembers. "She held the book in her hands when she was half asleep, eyes half open, just alive enough to have it register. And she smiled."

A remarkable story? Yes and no. The almost-instantaneous, professional-level production of Trigère's book would have been impossible just a few years before this. But starting in 2013, Ingram had made the near-miraculous technological capacities of Lightning Source available to practically anyone in the world through its new service, IngramSpark.

Dedicated to the needs of independent publishers and authors, IngramSpark offers a range of digital tools that make on-demand printing and book distribution easy and accessible for people even with minimal technical training and very modest resources. As Robin Cutler, director of IngramSpark, explains, "Our interface was streamlined and automated to create a better do-it-yourself experience—to provide a front door that's easy for an author or a small publisher to come through." IngramSpark books can be printed in quantities from one to hundreds or thousands, with unit prices starting at two or three dollars for a small paperback volume. With a few clicks of the mouse, the same books can be released for distribution through Ingram's own vast network of booksellers and other retailers as well as through countless online channels, including Amazon, BN.com, and many more.

IngramSpark has made Ingram a major force in one of the biggest burgeoning trends of the book business—self-publishing. No longer a euphemism for "vanity publishing," in which books undeserving of readership get published for pay, self-publishing has become a respectable and fast-growing corner of the industry. It's a trend driven, in part, by the consolidation among publishers we've previously discussed. With fewer commercial publishers operating independently, would-be authors without significant publicity platforms are finding it harder and harder to attract publishing contracts, even when their books would be of interest and value to at least a modest audience. Self-publishing is filling the gap.

A number of businesses have sprung up to support self-publishers. The two most important are Ingram's IngramSpark and Amazon's Kindle Direct Publishing. And while both of these POD giants offer quality service,

IngramSpark is uniquely valuable to independent authors because of Ingram's special place across the book industry. Many book retailers, especially small booksellers, are reluctant to do business with Amazon because of the competition the company poses. Ingram generates no such concern. So self-publishers who want the option of distribution through thousands of independent bookstores have made IngramSpark their partner of choice.

Within months of its launch in 2013, large numbers of independent publishers and authors began finding their way to IngramSpark. Positive word of mouth played the major role. Cutler reports:

> More and more people began using our services. We didn't even know how they heard about it. I remember just a few months after our launch, getting a note from someone saying, "Do you realize that Laila Ali, Muhammad Ali's daughter, has loaded a book onto IngramSpark?" Then Eriq La Salle, an actor famous for his role on the TV series *ER*, published a book through us. By early in 2014, we started seeing IngramSpark being listed as one of the top new publishing platforms. We didn't market that—it just happened organically.

By 2020, IngramSpark had grown into a business with over $100 million in annual revenues. It had helped publish more than seven million books, with four thousand new books added to its roster each day. The self-publishing revolution is yet another way that digital tools are transforming the centuries-old world of publishing—and once again, Ingram is in the forefront.

18

The Family Business, Today and Tomorrow

Now that we've traced the Ingram story from its earliest days to the present, it's natural to wonder what the future may bring. Of course, the world of business is inherently unpredictable, especially in tumultuous times like the present. But to a remarkable degree, as Ingram itself has demonstrated over the past quarter-century, even without access to a crystal ball, creative business thinkers can actually *create* the future.

The same has been true of pioneers in every age, from Johannes Gutenberg to James Watt, Eli Whitney to Nelson Rockefeller, Thomas Edison to Henry Ford, and Steve Jobs to Jeff Bezos. Each one possessed a special chemistry, combining the creative ability to see new combinations and possibilities with strategic insight, relentless focus, and limitless energy. Similar qualities can be seen in the intrapreneurial leaders of Ingram Book, especially John Ingram.

It's not possible to foresee in any detail what the next twenty-five or fifty years might bring for this business that has already played a major role in transforming its industry. No one knows that better than John himself:

> The life of this company has always been more about a journey than a destination, and it has certainly evolved over time. We've had twists and turns over our first fifty years, and I expect there will be twists and turns to come. But I am hopeful we will always remain relevant and profitable, known for our excellent team and outstanding service, and always prepared to take advantage of the opportunities that come our way.
>
> Some might say that Ingram has been lucky. Maybe so. But I believe that luck is the intersection of preparation with opportunity. So I hope we stay lucky, and the next fifty years will take care of itself.

As John suggests, Ingram's "luck" is largely a matter of preparation—having the intelligence, clarity, and resources to recognize and take advantage of opportunities as they arise, and to do so in a way that creates powerful streams of value both for Ingram and for its countless business partners. But the qualities that make Ingram special go even deeper than these gifts, important as they are. Ingram's story is a story of remarkable business creativity, technological innovation, strategic insight, and adroit leadership. But it's also the story of a family business driven to an unusual extent by generous *human* values.

From the company's very beginning, the idea of family has had special meaning for most Ingram associates, whatever their assignments and wherever they worked, from the warehouse floor to the corporate headquarters. Of course, in the literal sense, Ingram has always been a family business: Bronson Ingram, his wife Martha, and their children have been both owners of the business and, to varying degrees, active participants in building and guiding its operations.

Far from being distant shareholders mainly interested in cashing dividend checks, the Ingrams—especially Bronson and his son John—have brought impressive managerial insight, tough-minded decision-making, and intrapreneurial drive to the daily workings of the company. And as we've seen, Martha also played a unique and powerful role as the company's informal ombudsman, forging a deeply personal connection between the frontline associates and the executive leadership that contributed enormously to Ingram's reputation as a great place to work. "Martha never stopped listening to people," says YS Chi, the longtime Ingram executive who now is an Ingram board member. "She never judged, she never jumped to conclusions. She's the most generous human being I have ever met."

The personal presence of the Ingrams has left a powerful stamp on the organization in other ways. For decades, the Ingram family has also been an important force in the civic, charitable, and social life of their community.

As a prominent Nashville leader in her own right, Martha Ingram worked through the 1970s leading the civic effort in Nashville to develop the Tennessee Performing Arts Center (TPAC), the downtown home of the Nashville Symphony Orchestra, Nashville Ballet, Nashville Opera, Tennessee Repertory Theatre, and Circle Players. Later, Bronson invited Martha to join the family business as director of public affairs, including coordination of Ingram's charitable work.

Bronson was also involved in a range of charitable activities. The deepest of his philanthropic connections was with Vanderbilt University, an important institution for Nashville and for the entire state of Tennessee.

Throughout his life, Bronson maintained the family connection with Vanderbilt that his father had started. Bronson joined the Vanderbilt board in 1967 and became the board's president in 1991. One of his major accomplishments in that role was chairing the six-year-long Campaign for Vanderbilt, which achieved the lofty goal of raising $500 million for the university's endowment. It was a huge task that he tackled with gusto and dedication remarkable for a man who was simultaneously guiding the fortunes of a large family business as well as engaging in other important civic tasks.

In 1993, Bronson also launched the Ingram Scholars Program, designed to support students with financial need who (as the university's website explains) "demonstrate a willingness and ability to combine a successful business or professional career with a lifelong commitment to finding solutions to critical problems facing modern society." Ingram Scholars engage in community outreach projects even while maintaining a serious academic workload, thereby developing habits of giving back to society that most of them maintain throughout their productive lifetimes. Many have gone on to have highly successful careers in business.

Bronson served as president of the Vanderbilt board until his death in 1995. In 1999, Martha became the first female chairman of the VU board. Their sons Orrin and John have also served on the university's board and, together with their siblings David B. Ingram and Robin Ingram Patton, continue to be active VU supporters.

When Ingram Micro, the family's privately held microcomputer software distribution business, was taken public in 1996, the Ingram Charitable Fund made a gift to Vanderbilt of company shares then valued at more than $300 million. At the time, it constituted the largest gift to any university in US history.

When the family whose name adorns the company is dedicated to selfless giving on this scale, it makes a palpable difference to the culture of the organization.

It also makes a difference when the family acts out the same values in the way it treats the people who work at the company. Ingram veterans retell many stories about thoughtful, generous deeds by members of the family—like the night when Harry Hoffman's teenage daughter, battling psychological demons, called him to say that she was in jail in a little town some three hundred miles from home. Distraught, Hoffman phoned Bronson, looking for advice. "I'll have a plane ready in a few minutes," Bronson told him. Within a couple of hours, Hoffman's daughter was safe at home. "That was one of the most wonderful things that has ever been done for me," Hoffman recalls.

Other acts, smaller but equally significant, have helped shape the unique corporate culture of Ingram. One is the consistent use of the term "associates" to refer to Ingram employees. This is now a fairly common usage in American corporations, but Ingram was among the first companies to adopt it. Many company veterans credit Phil Pfeffer with popularizing the word.

"It was intended to convey respect," Pfeffer explains. "At Ingram, we are respectful associates of one another. No job is more important than any other. The person who is on the line making the cartons to ship the book orders has a job that is critical to the success of the company. And so does everyone else on the organization chart. The quality of work that each of us does reflects on everything we do."

Sharon Hillman Fields echoes the sentiment. She was an Ingram associate from the time of her college graduation until her retirement thirty-nine years later. She joined the company as a freight clerk in June 1976, during the time of the Raymar acquisition; she retired in 2015 as vice president and controller. She is one of many Ingram associates who speak of Ingram as "a family business" both in terms of its ownership and its esprit de corps.

"The 1970s and 1980s were a time of heavy growth for the company," Fields recalls, "but as a young person I could see that hard work and dedication were rewarded by the Ingram family. We had a strong bond that was built during those days of working together as a team. Management led by example. We were all just working together, no one more important than another. Oh, what a great feeling of accomplishment we all had at the success of the company, because we were all considered part of the team. Our blood ran Ingram blue, you might say."

Mary Willene "Willie" Collins, a retired manager in Ingram's telephone sales section, shares similar memories: "It was so special in the early days. We were just some good people doing some good things back then. John Ingram knew everybody by name, and Mr. and Mrs. Ingram were friendly and just the best people. Their business philosophy was to treat everybody the way they wanted to be treated, so then everybody treated the customers the same way. That started with Mr. and Mrs. Ingram. We just formed a big ol' family."

Speaking as a member of the founding family, John says it this way: "There's not a first-class section and a tourist section at Ingram. That's what the word "associate" is about. Maybe that's one reason a lot of people end up marrying someone they met at Ingram."

From early in its history, Ingram Industries has been "a family of families." Many married couples hold positions in different Ingram divisions. A husband might work for Ingram Barge Company, for instance, while his wife is employed at Ingram Book.

The philosophy of treating associates "like family" extends beyond personal gestures of respect and appreciation. Mike Lovett describes it this way: "The Ingram businesses exhibit an exemplary culture and live their values. Ingram associates care for the Ingram family, and the family cares for their associates." He offered this concrete example:

When Ingram Micro went public, the Ingram Industries shares in the associates' 401(k) accounts were converted to Ingram Micro shares. This made millionaires out of a number of long-term associates, from boat captains and secretaries to sales people and cooks. I remember Bronson saying, "All the Ingram people who worked so hard to provide the resources to make Ingram Micro possible should now participate in the rewards." The way the company acted on that belief illustrates a commitment to shared values not found anywhere else I know.

The Ingram Micro public offering is not the only illustration of the company's commitment to sharing the fruits of success with its associates. It's no accident that Ingram boasts an unusually large number of longtime employees—people who joined the company as young, ambitious businesspeople, rose steadily to positions of influence and authority, and remained with Ingram for twenty years, thirty years, and even longer. This has happened so often because the company offers talented individuals the things they value most: fair compensation, the opportunity to develop their skills, a steady stream of interesting challenges, the freedom to experiment and innovate, and respect as individuals and colleagues. The Ingram approach to people management explains how a relatively little-known company based in Nashville, Tennessee, has been able to compete successfully for brilliant creative talent in an era seemingly dominated by headline-grabbing digital giants like Microsoft, Google, Netflix, Facebook, and Amazon.

Thus, Ingram is one of a handful of great American companies that demonstrate how treating people well is not just the right thing to do—it's also the smartest way to run a business.

Lovett sums it up this way: "At Ingram, the family name is always over the door. And that's because it's a family business, with family values they really live by, and that they share with everyone they work with. That's what makes it a special company."

Whatever new challenges and opportunities the coming decades may hold for Ingram as a trend-setting leader in the book business, it seems likely that the deep-rooted values that make the company a great place to work and serve, to experiment and learn, and to grow and thrive will remain strong. If that happens, the next fifty years of Ingram history will bring new stories of remarkable innovation that we can only dimly imagine today, offering powerful benefits to the publishers, authors, booksellers, librarians, educators, students, and readers of tomorrow.

Acknowledgments

In my efforts to understand this extraordinary story, I am indebted to many good people who shared with me their time, help, and firsthand knowledge, together with much patience. This involved delving into personal memories, private notes, archived materials in libraries private and public, and many keepsake photos.

First, as ever, for their patience and tolerance of my disappearances into the writing room, I am grateful to my family and especially to Marsha.

To interview seventy-nine people, many of them over multiple sittings, I thank the dozen executive assistants who scheduled visits, arranging either quiet rooms or telephone time with their bosses: Lisa Presley, Alex Burlason, Phyllis Reid, Nita Shoemake, Susan Rich, Lisa Chalfant, Karan Pugh, Kathi Reagh, Alicia Rice, Mike Cook, Becky Jones, and Pam Garrison. My thanks also to Sue Harvey, who served John Ingram over many years in times of transition.

For their assistance in collecting the data and photographs that inform and illustrate this story, I am especially grateful to Ingram's Wayne Keegan, Phil Ollila, Judy Allen, Brian McKinley, Marilyn Dick, and Kris Wiese.

Philip Nagy and Kathy Smith, in the Special Collections Department of Vanderbilt University Library, provided access to the archival photos of Hank Ingram, Bronson Ingram, and Jack Stambaugh that appear on these pages. Other photos were kindly shared by the Nashville historian David Ewing from his private collection.

Madeleine Donovan, on our extraordinary team at The Strategy Group in Nashville, was essential to helping build this photo collection and managing it over many months to the point of publication.

For my understanding of the early history of the Tennessee Performing Arts Center, I thank Mac Pirkle, Jennifer Turner, and Roberta Ciuffo West.

The participation of Mike Shatzkin was invaluable to this project, especially his help in securing interviews with leaders in the complicated publishing and bookselling trades. Mike was involved in many of our interviews, and brought his deep knowledge of the book industry and its long and winding history. He enriched my understanding of much you have read in the preceding pages.

So also have Bruce Harris and Karl Weber, with their long experiences at a high level in publishing and professional editing, respectively. They turned my manuscript into this book, and sincerest thanks to them both.

I am grateful especially to all the families and many Ingram retirees who helped me with access to loved ones and their own memories of former colleagues who have passed. My special thanks to Art Carson, Michael Zibart, Margaret Zibart, Margaret Howell, Catherine Hoffman, Ann Mapp, Patti Freeman, Sharon Fields, and also Willie Collins, who brought me her scrapbook of notes, memoranda, and snapshots.

Finally, this result could never have been achieved in its candor and fullness without the complete trust, good humor, and large spirit of John Ingram.

Keel Hunt
Nashville, Tennessee
August 2020

Timeline of Ingram History

1928   O. H. (Hank) Ingram, a businessman based in Eau Claire, Wisconsin, purchases the Nashville-based Tennessee Tufting Company. Within a decade, he and his family will move to Nashville, which becomes the center of the family business.

1963   Hank Ingram dies. His sons Fritz and Bronson inherit the family businesses.

1964   Bronson Ingram and Jack Stambaugh purchase Tennessee Book Company for $245,000, making it a unit of Ingram Corp.

1970   Ingram Book Company is formed. As president, Harry Hoffman expands the company's offerings from textbooks for Tennessee public schools to supplying library collections and retail bookstores in the southeastern United States.

1972   The Ingram Microfiche Reader is introduced, giving retail booksellers weekly updates on titles currently available in Ingram inventory.

1975   Digital ordering system launched with toll-free access to the Ingram call center. First issue of *Advance* magazine is published.

1976   Ingram Book acquires a national footprint by buying Pasadena-based wholesaler Raymar Book Company.

1977   Philip M. Pfeffer joins Ingram Book as director of financial planning.

1978   Ingram Corp. is reorganized into Ingram Industries Inc., with Bronson Ingram as chairman. Hoffman departs Ingram to become CEO of Waldenbooks. Pfeffer is named president and CEO of Ingram Book Company.

1979   First mainframe computer installed at Ingram headquarters in La Vergne, Tennessee.

1980   Pfeffer is named executive VP of Ingram Industries and CEO of Ingram Book Group. David Williams is named president of the Book Company unit.

1981   Bronson and Pfeffer explore prospects for supplying non-book products, especially computer software and movie videocassettes, to retail bookstores. Ingram Library Services is established.

1983   Steven Mason is appointed president of Ingram Book Company.

1985   Ingram opens its first super warehouse at La Vergne.

1986 Flashback ordering tool for booksellers is introduced. Ingram acquires microcomputer products distributor Micro D and renames it Ingram Micro Inc. Ingram Periodicals Inc. is launched.

1987 Ingram Library Services is launched.

1989 Lee Synnott is named chairman and CEO of Ingram Book Group.

1990 Second super warehouse is opened in Fort Wayne, Indiana.

1994 Third super warehouse is opened in Roseburg, Oregon.

1995 Bronson Ingram dies. Martha R. Ingram becomes chairman of Ingram Industries Inc.

1996 John Ingram is named chairman of Ingram Book Group. Incorporation of Lightning Print Inc. Tennessee. Initial public offering of shares in Ingram Micro.

1997 Ingram Book acquires Spring Arbor Distributors, serving Christian bookstores. Mike Lovett is named CEO of Ingram Book Group. David Ingram takes Ingram Entertainment Inc. independent.

1998 Lightning Print Inc. is launched, providing print-on-demand services to book publishers. Ingram launches ipage, a web-based merchandising tool for booksellers. Ingram and Barnes & Noble announce agreement for B&N to acquire Ingram Book Group, subject to regulatory approval.

1999 John is named chairman of Ingram Book Group and vice chairman of Ingram Industries Inc. board of directors. Federal regulators balk at the proposed sale of Ingram to Barnes & Noble, and the deal is withdrawn.

2000 Lightning Source (formerly Lightning Print Inc.) produces its millionth book. Ingram enters new business relationships with Microsoft, Adobe, and leading publishers for ebook and other digital content fulfillment services.

2001 Fourth super warehouse is opened in Chambersburg, Pennsylvania, including a consolidated returns center. Lightning Source opens new print facility in the United Kingdom.

2003 Lightning Source produces its ten millionth book.

2004 Ingram Publisher Services is established, offering sales, marketing, and distribution services for publishers. James (Jim) E. Chandler is named CEO of Ingram Book Group. Lightning Source UK prints its millionth book.

2005 CoreSource is launched, offering digital asset management systems for book publishers and other content creators.

2006 Ingram acquires VitalSource Technologies, Coutts Information Services, and MyiLibrary. Lightning Source prints its twenty-five millionth book.

2007 Lightning Source opens new POD facility in Allentown, Pennsylvania. VitalSource distributes its billionth ebook.

2008 John is elected chairman of Ingram Industries board. David (Skip) Prichard is named CEO of Ingram Book Group.

2009 Ingram consolidates management of Ingram Book, Lightning Source, and Ingram Digital. Lightning Source enters joint venture with Hachette Livre France to offer print-on-demand services to the French book market.

2010 Ingram expands into Asia-Pacific market with announcement to establish a Lightning Source operation in Australia.

2011 Ingram launches Global CONNECT to connect print and distribution with local book manufacturers, beginning in Brazil and Germany. CoreSource distributes its millionth product.

2012 John is named chairman and CEO of Ingram Content Group. Lightning Source launches full-color book printing and opens POD facility in Fairfield, Ohio.

2013 IngramSpark on-demand publishing platform is launched.

2014 Ingram's VitalSource Technologies acquires CourseSmart. Lightning Sources opens automated POD facility in Fresno, California. IngramSpark grows to 10,000 customers

2015 Ingram Publisher Services distributes its first *New York Times* No. 1 bestseller. Ingram's VitalSource now is in more than 7,000 educational institutions across 241 countries and territories. Ingram opens new 300,000-square-foot textbook warehouse in Antioch, Tennessee.

2016 Shawn Morin is named CEO of Ingram Content Group. In a deal with Perseus Books, Ingram acquires distribution businesses and distribution center in Jackson, Tennessee. Ingram Academic Services is launched.

2017 Ingram acquires Verba, Thrivist, NBN International, OptiQly, and Intrepid.

2018   IngramSpark distributes its first *New York Times* bestseller. Ingram acquires Acrobatiq.

2019   Ingram Content opens new distribution center in Milton Keynes, United Kingdom. New Lightning Source production facility opens in Jackson, Tennessee.

2020   VitalSource and its associated publishers give students affected by COVID-19 pandemic free access to e-textbooks. Ingram launches Bookfinity.com to help consumers select books and connect directly with online retailers. Five of the *New York Times* top ten nonfiction paperback bestsellers are supplied by Ingram's Guaranteed Availability Program. Lightning Source US orders average one million units per week in the March–June period. Ingram invests $6 million in new equipment for its Lightning Source operations in the United States, the United Kingdom, and Australia.

Key Data on Ingram Growth

Annual Revenues for Ingram Content Group, 1970-2020
in millions of dollars

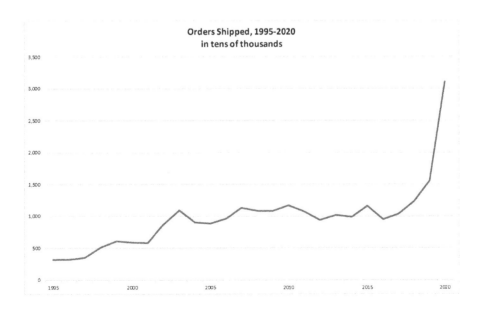

Orders Shipped, 1995-2020
in tens of thousands

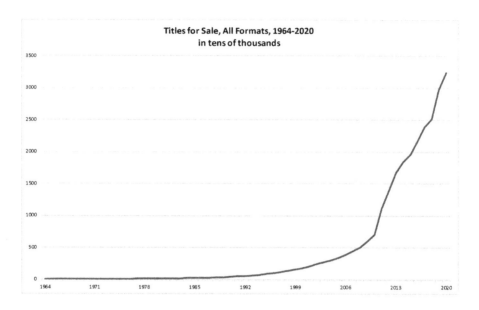

Titles for Sale, All Formats, 1964-2020
in tens of thousands

List of Interviewees

The story of Ingram's first fifty years is only partly found in its founding corporate documents and the news coverage by the industry trade press. The more extensive record lives in the memories of Ingram associates, past and present, and in the recollections of industry leaders who have held special vantage points across the book trade over time.

Over the past two years, the seventy-nine individuals named alphabetically below have generously shared their memories of Ingram's rise at its various stages of development, growth, and diversification. The conversations thus ranged from warehouse and call-center associates, financial managers and field sales reps, the line executives who at each step along the way imagined the future, and publishers and booksellers.

All these, from their varied perspectives, came to know Ingram best as the size and influence of this family business grew through its first half-century.

Lamar Alexander
Judy Allen
Kelley Maier Anderson
Ted Baylis
J. Kirby Best
Dennis C. Bottorff
Larry Brewster
Art Carson
Jim Chandler
YS Chi
Phil Clark
Tom Clarkson
Peter Clifton
Suzanne Close
Willie Collins
Ken Cope
David Cully
Robin Cutler
Frank Daniels III

Brian Dauphin
Peter Dougherty
Morgan Entrekin
Shawn Everson
Sharon Hillman Fields
Mike Fine
Sue Flaster
Kent Freeman
Patti Pigg Freeman
Bruce Harris
Sue Harvey
Aubrey Harwell
Dick Heffernan
Harry Hoffman
Michael Holdsworth
Randy Hooper
Margaret Howell
Shannon Hunt
David B. Ingram

John R. Ingram
Martha R. Ingram
Orrin H. Ingram
Bill Jones
George Kaludis
Wayne Keegan
Chip Lacy
Steve Little
Mike Lovett
Ann Mapp
Ed Marino
Charles Marshall
Steven Mason
Janet McDonald
Bill Morelli
Shawn Morin
Ed Morrow
Arnaud Nourry
Phil Ollila
Peter Osnos
Richard Patton

Robin Ingram Patton
Phil Pfeffer
Buddy Pickler
Mac Pirkle
Craig Pollock
John Reed
Kenneth L. Roberts
David Roland
Jack Romanos
Lavona Russell
Johnny Secrest
Mike Shatzkin
George Stanley
Lee Synnott
David Taylor
Ron Watson
Emily Weiss
E. W. (Bud) Wendell
Tom Wright
Michael Zibart

BIBLIOGRAPHY

Anderson, Chris. "The Long Tail." *Wired*, October 1, 2004.
———. *The Long Tail: Why the Future of Business Is Selling Less of More*. New York: Hyperion, 2006.
Bosman, Julie. "Times Will Rank E-Book Best Sellers." *New York Times*, November 10, 2010.
Carey, Bill. *Fortunes, Fiddles and Fried Chicken: A Nashville Business History*. Nashville: Hillsboro Press, 2000.
Chappell, Lindsay. "Bronson Ingram: The Limelight of Public Concern." *Advantage Magazine*, April 1987.
Culver, Donna. *Tribute to Bronson Ingram, Interviews with Family, Friends and Community Leaders*, May 1995. Produced on assignment of Vanderbilt Chancellor Joe B. Wyatt for the Ingram Scholars Program.
Deal, Terrence E., and Allan A. Kennedy. *Corporate Cultures: The Rites and Rituals of Corporate Life*. New York: Basic Books, 1982.
Eaton, Leslie. "E. Bronson Ingram, Who Built Family Concern Into Giant, 63." *New York Times*, June 21, 1995.
Gaw, Jonathan. "The Spine Behind the Ingram Empire." *Los Angeles Times*, June 6, 1999.
Hawn, Carleen. "Sibling Rivalry." *Forbes*, September 6, 1999.
Hoffman, Harry. *The Pocket Mentor: Essential Advice for Aspiring Executives*. Kansas City: Andrews McMeel Publishers, 1998.
Hunt, Keel. *Crossing the Aisle*. Nashville: Vanderbilt University Press, 2018.
Ingram, Martha Rivers. *E. Bronson Ingram: Complete These Unfinished Tasks of Mine*. Nashville: Martha Ingram, 2001.
———, with D. B. Kellogg. *Apollo's Struggle: A Performing Arts Odyssey in the Athens of the South, Nashville, Tennessee*. Nashville: Hillsboro Press, 2004.
Kellogg, D. B. *Martha Rivers Ingram: No Ordinary Lady*. Nashville: Tiger Club Press, 2008.
———. *Martha Rivers Ingram: Celebrating the Arts*. Nashville: Tiger Club Press, 2016.
Lane, Randall. "A Tale of Two Brothers." *Forbes*, October 24, 1994.
Lewis, Princine. "New Commons Residence Halls Named for Former Vice Chancellor, BOT Member." *Vanderbilt Register*, December 4, 2006.
Marino, Edward J. *The Loyalty Payoff, Building Loyalty to Boost Profits*. NAPL (National Association for Printing Leadership), 2005.

McDowell, Edwin. "The Book Industry's Bestselling Middleman." *New York Times*, July 8, 1984.

Pinchot, Gilbert. "Who Is the Intrapreneur?" in *Intrapreneuring: Why You Don't Have to Leave the Corporation to Become an Entrepreneur*. New York: Harper & Row, 1984.

Publishing Trends Editors. "The Ingram Empire: Ingram Book Group Scans for Growth, As Rivals Grab Core Market Share." *Publishing Trends*, March 1, 2003.

Quint, Barbara. "Barnes & Noble Abandons Attempt to Buy Ingram." *Information Today*, June 28, 1999.

Segal, David. "Barnes & Noble Drops Ingram Deal." *Washington Post*, June 3, 1999.

Shatzkin, Leonard. *In Cold Type: Overcoming the Book Crisis*. Boston: Houghton Mifflin Harcourt, 1982.

Shatzkin, Mike. "Second Old Publishing Story: The First Great Book Supply Chain Tech Disruption." *The Shatzkin Files* (The Idea Logical Company), March 7, 2009.

——————. "The Supply Chain for Book Publishing is Being Changed by Coronavirus too." *The Shatzkin Files* (The Idea Logical Company), April 19, 2020.

——————. "Surprise!" *The Shatzkin Files* (The Idea Logical Company), June 1, 1996.

Shatzkin, Mike, and Robert Paris Riger. *The Book Business: What Everyone Needs to Know*. Oxford: Oxford University Press, 2019.

Slywotzky, Adrian, with Karl Weber. *Demand: Creating What People Love Before They Know They Want It*. New York: Crown Business, 2011.

Teicher, Craig Morgan. "Change Makers: John Ingram, Guiding the Family Company into a New Era." *Publishers Weekly*, June 29, 2009.

Trigère, Jane. *What's a Grandparent?* South Deerfield, MA: Schoen Books, 2018.

Twining, Charles E. *Downriver: Orrin H. Ingram and The Empire Lumber Company*. The State Historical Society of Wisconsin, 1975.

Index

Page locators in *italics* indicate photographs.

Photo Credits and Permissions

ABOUT THE AUTHOR

KEEL HUNT is the author of two books on Tennessee political history: *Coup: The Day the Democrats Ousted Their Governor, Put Republican Lamar Alexander in Office Early, and Stopped a Pardon Scandal* (2017), and *Crossing the Aisle: How Bipartisanship Brought Tennessee to the Twenty-First Century and Could Save America* (2018), both published by Vanderbilt University Press. He has been a columnist for the USA Today Tennessee network since 2013. In his early career, he was a journalist and Washington correspondent. He has been an adviser to the Ingram family and Ingram businesses since 1995. Read more about him at www.KeelHunt.com.

Photo credit: Olivia Hunt

CPSIA information can be obtained
at www.ICGtesting.com
Printed in the USA
BVHW091916230421
605647BV00001B/1/J